David S. G. Goodman is Director of the Institute for International Studies, University of Technology, Sydney. He is the author of *Deng Xiaoping and the Chinese Revolution* (Routledge, 1994). Other recent publications include (with Beverley Hooper) *China's Quiet Revolution* (Longman Cheshire, 1994) and (with Richard Robison) *The New Rich in Asia* (Routledge, 1995).

Gerald Segal is Senior Fellow in Asian Security Studies at the International Institute for Strategic Studies and Director of the ESRC's Pacific Asia Programme. He was founder and first editor of *The Pacific Review*. His recent publications include *China Changes Shape* (Adelphi Paper No. 287, 1994) and *The Fate of Hong Kong* (Simon & Schuster, 1993).

The authors' joint publications include: *The China Challenge* (Routledge, Chatham House Papers, 1986), *China at Forty* (Oxford University Press, 1989), *China in the Nineties* (Oxford University Press, 1991) and *China Deconstructs* (Routledge, 1994).

IMPRINT
Abroad

CHINA WITHOUT DENG

David S. G. Goodman
& Gerald Segal

Editions Tom Thompson
Sydney New York Amsterdam

An IMPRINT book
Imprint is a division of Editions Tom Thompson
11 Cove Street, Watsons Bay, Sydney, NSW 2030, Australia

Distributed by
HarperCollins *Publishers*
25 Ryde Road, Pymble, Sydney, NSW 2073, Australia
31 View Road, Glenfield, Auckland 10, New Zealand
HarperCollins *International*
10 East 53rd Street, New York, NY 10022, USA
In de Knipscheer *Uitgeverij*
Singel 450, 1017 Av Amsterdam

ISBN 1 875892 03 6

Cover design: Robyn Latimer
Printed in Australia by Griffin Paperbacks, Adelaide

Contents

'As long as we, the older generation, are still around ... the hostile forces know that change cannot happen. But who can guarantee this once we old people pass away?'

Deng Xiaoping, 1992

Introduction

What Deng Xiaoping's death means for China

THE death of Deng Xiaoping is arguably more important than that of any other world leader since Mao Zedong went to meet Marx in September 1976. Deng was the 'paramount leader' of the world's fastest growing major economy and the country touted as the driving force behind the coming Pacific Century. In pluralist political systems the death of one leader may not matter as much because there are effective mechanisms for succession, but in a highly personalized, non-institutionalised and consequently uncertain political system like China's, the death of a leader matters a great deal. Deng was also both the tangible manifestation of China's revolutionary past and the prime proponent of its modernising future. His death presents the People's Republic of China [PRC] with a major challenge.

Deng's importance in setting China on its reforming course is undeniable, but his major impact was already achieved well before his death. Deng can be credited with having ensured that China began sweeping market-oriented reforms and persisted when many

1

thought it might turn back. But having embarked on and sustained such far-reaching reforms Deng discovered, well before his death, that the reforms soon took on a life of their own. Once power was decentralized it was very hard if not impossible to claw back. Once the Chinese Communist Party [CCP] empowered individuals and collectives to pursue their own interests and local policies, the Central authorities could no longer control key parts of the Chinese economy or even its society and political system. Similarly, Deng had dug a course for Chinese foreign relations that, once entrenched by the mid-1990s, became inescapable. China's interdependence with the world, in terms of its need for foreign markets, energy or food, was vital to sustain domestic growth. For Deng's successors, undoing the economic reforms or ending the interdependence with the outside world are not real options.

The reform era initiated by Deng Xiaoping and the CCP is full of fundamental paradoxes. The CCP has started a process of change that will of necessity undermine its own position; it has set in motion processes it needs to control but ultimately cannot. If it tries to stop these processes then it will ensure political conflict sooner rather than later. Though in the short term the CCP could undoubtedly bring the gradual processes of transition to a halt, it would just as undoubtedly jeopardise its own position; its legitimacy would be irreparably damaged.

However, if the CCP does not also successfully manage the transition it has set in motion, the situation in general may easily become ungovernable, and its own position would again be jeopardised. In short, though a CCP may survive in some form or other, there is no future for the CCP of the past and the political system it created — the structural imperatives for change are just too great. There might be a conservative backlash in the short-term, but the longer-term prospects are for continuing change: polycentrism, regionalism and even possibly some form of democratisation.

Deng Xiaoping's success in launching reform had begun to produce tough choices for China well before his death. Once the rising expectations of economic reform gathered strength, the rulers could no longer risk a strategy that might stop the growth. In order to maintain power, economic reform required that more power be decentralized. As this happened, the rulers pretended to rule and the ruled pretended to be ruled. As economic growth required greater openness to the outside world, China even found that the international market economy also assumed greater control over the fate of China.

It was a paradox of this economic power that, as China grew richer and apparently stronger, it only did so as that power became less concentrated and more diffuse — shared throughout the country and with others abroad. The challenge for Deng's successors is how to rule at home — and in effect to redefine the meaning of 'rule' — and interact with the outside world, under these new and difficult conditions. The problem is compounded by the fact that the challenge will have to be met without the advantage of a powerful and ruthless leader like Deng.

More immediately it might be thought that the death of Deng matters less because we already know the formal succession. Deng Xiaoping held no formal positions after 1989, and there are therefore no immediate surprises about who follows him in nominal positions of power. Unlike other successions in states ruled by Communist Parties, the outside world knows who is President, Party leader, and who is on the Politbureau.

Yet few observers of China are taken in by the fact that the formal place-holders are already positioned. Most know that power in China is highly personalized, and that Deng, for all his physical and mental incapacities in his dying days, remained the leading political power in China. It was Deng who sanctioned the crack-down in 1989 and who revived the economic reforms in the early 1990s. His death may not leave a vacuum in formal terms, but it does in terms of who, if anyone, fills the void of political authority.

China will have no paramount leader for some time to come, if ever again. The new leader or even leaders of China will be from the post-revolutionary generation and therefore have far less authority. Within a very short period even that generation — born for the most part during the late 1920s and already quite old — will be superseded by a still younger generation of leaders. The succession ding-dong after Deng will be at least a two-phase event and experience suggests that the 'chosen successor' rarely holds power for long. The outside world is likely to be talking about power struggles in China for many years to come, despite every effort made by the Chinese authorities to suggest that there is nothing to worry about. The line-up of leaders we now see is only in place because Deng put them there, and this was only after a lengthy bargaining process with other elderly revolutionary leaders. With Deng's death, the survivors will be more free to struggle among themselves. The combination of an already ageing successor generation within the leadership and uninstitutionalised politics is not a formula for political stability.

In an important sense it matters less who succeeds Deng given that Deng's successors will be far less powerful than he was. Deng has unleashed such compelling forces of reform that no successor can manage the process in the ways once exercised by the CCP. As market forces are introduced and regional leaders assume increasingly important power, China can no longer be ruled by a ruthless Communist Party from a single centre. Because the clock of reform cannot be turned back, governing China will be even more difficult and less centralized than during the Deng era.

Who will replace Deng?

The Usual Suspects

THE formally designated successor is President (and General Secretary of the Communist Party) Jiang Zemin, who is also nominal head of the military. Born in July 1926 in Jiangsu Province, he first achieved fame in the 1950s as a deputy director of the Shanghai Soap Factory. In 1955 he served as a trainee at the Stalin Automobile Factory in Moscow. He worked in various ministries in Beijing in the 1970s and 1980s until he became Mayor of Shanghai in July 1985. In 1987 he joined the Party's Politbureau but in June 1989 was anointed as Party General Secretary. In November he had become the all-important chairman of the Military Commission of the Party.

Jiang has John Major-like qualities of charisma and, like Mr Major, took power in the midst of a major upheaval in the old leadership. There is little in his background to suggest a man of ideas or a true believer in reform. Jiang is a place-holder and few observers give him much chance of surviving when the real struggle for power begins. He is formally in charge of the armed forces but lacks any military experience and has none of Deng's ties of loyalties to the armed forces that were so crucial in earlier power struggles.

The next putative successor, Prime Minister Li Peng, is usually given even less chance of success in the medium term. Li was born in October 1928 in Chengdu,

Sichuan Province. His parents were Communist Party martyrs and he was 'adopted' by Zhou Enlai, the deified former Prime Minister under Mao.

Li spent six years from 1948 at the Moscow Power Institute and on his return to China spent more than 30 years working his way up the bureaucracy of the power industry and the Party. He became a Vice Premier in 1982, a member of the Politbureau in 1985, and joined the Politbureau's Standing Committee in 1987. He took over as Prime Minister in April 1988 in the wake of a leadership struggle. During the crisis of 1989, Li was identified as the arch-conservative anxious to crush opposition and opposed to the more liberal Party leader Zhao Ziyang.

In subsequent years he has had both heart trouble and political trouble as the wave of reform seemed to leave him on the political sidings. But he remains far more resilient and crafty than many foreigners suggest. He obviously has powerful backers in the Party and is well positioned to play a more prominent role should the succession take place when the economic reforms stumble. He is not loved by the armed forces either, but they did defend his rule in 1989 and therefore have a stake in the 'verdict' on the events of 1989 not being overturned.

The man snapping at Li Peng's heels is Vice-Premier Zhu Rongji. Born in 1928 in Changsha, Hunan Province and graduated from the Electric Motor Engine Department of the Qinghua University, he toiled in state ministries but apparently suffered for expressing liberal views during the late 1950s. In 1978 he became Director of a liberal think-tank (Industrial Economics Institute) where he made important contacts with reformers and their ideas.

7

By the late 1980s he had moved into Party jobs in Shanghai. In April 1988 he became Mayor of Shanghai and took over the top Party job in the city when Jiang Zemin was moved to Beijing after the traumatic events of 1989. Zhu and Jiang masterminded the effective suppression of unrest in 1989 with far less bloodshed than in Beijing. Zhu in particular cultivated an image as a reformer. He travelled outside China promoting his city and expressing private opinions that were more moderate than the official hardline. In Shanghai he was known as 'one chop Zhu' for his ability to cut through the bureaucracy. He became a Vice Premier in 1991 and a member of the seven-man Politbureau Standing Committee in 1992.

In March 1993 he became China's senior Vice Premier in an attempt to get a grip on an economy spiralling out of control. Although he has failed to regain control of an economy now driven by market forces and decentralized to coastal authority, he retains his reputation as 'China's Gorbachev' and the man most likely to take China down a reformist path after Deng. But Zhu's failure to get a grip on the economy undermines his authority in the longer term and suggests that the post-Deng leaders will have even less control than many thought. Zhu may have made his move to the top just that little bit too soon.

Until the meteoric rise of Zhu Rongji, the most sparkling star in the firmament was Li Ruihuan, currently in charge of ideology in a de-ideologizing state. Li was born in 1935 in Tianjin, another of the major coastal cities providing potential future leaders for China. First trained as a carpenter, he emerged through the building materials industry in the Beijing area and began the reform era in the Tianjin Party structure. He became mayor in 1983 after

8

having won a Central Committee seat in the National Party in 1982. He joined the Politbureau of the Party in 1987 and the Standing Committee in June 1989.

In many respects Li Ruihuan is a better fit for the profile of a Chinese Gorbachev than Zhu Rongji. He is a little younger, has run a more reform-minded city, and has avoided the risks of a high-profile job before the succession to Deng takes place. As propaganda chief in recent years he has kept open contacts to more conservative elements, and yet earned points as a liberalizer. If Zhu Rongji does rise to the top after Deng, Mr Li is well placed to play a supporting role. But should Zhu stumble, as he appears to be at the moment, Li Ruihuan is the man to watch from the current batch of leaders.

An even younger member of the Politbureau's Standing Committee is Hu Jintao. Hu was born in 1942 in Anhui Province and graduated from the Water Conservation Department of Qinghua University. He has held posts in Beijing ministries, as well as in Gansu and Guizhou Provinces. During his time in the Party's Youth League he attached himself to the coat-tails of the liberal Party General Secretary Hu Yaobang whose death in 1989 sparked the student uprising.

Hu Jintao's service in China's more remote provinces apparently made him well suited to take over the sensitive job of Party chief in Tibet in 1988. He joined the Central Committee in 1985 and has been a swing member of the Politbureau's Standing Committee in the early 1990s. Among the younger but still senior leaders, Hu remains the more acceptable face of caution and slower reform. If the reforms stall and the older conservatives such as Li Peng are seen as too controversial to appoint,

Hu Jintao may well step forward.

Youth is of course a relative concept in China where bath-chair revolutionaries make even those in their seventies seem sprightly. In this political culture it would be unwise to eliminate from consideration those elderly leaders who still retain many of their mental marbles. Most notable in this category must be Yang Shangkun, the former President of China and a man with impressive connections in the armed forces. Yang was born in 1907 in Sichuan, studied in Moscow in the 1920s, fought revolutionary battles and took part in leadership struggles in the pre-1949 Party. His connections in the provinces include years as a leader in Guangdong province. His connections with the armed forces include many years as effectively in charge of the Party's Central Military Commission. Yang has been a close confidant of Deng since the late 1930s, as well as more recently a relative through marriage.

Yang is obviously not a long-term successor to Deng, but if his health holds he can play a crucial role after Deng dies. During the tumultuous events of 1989, Yang helped Deng keep a grip on power and deliver the armed forces in fighting order. Yang seems to have over-reached himself in the period after 1989 but has retained an active role in politics as well as various bridges to the disgraced former Party leader, Zhao Ziyang. Yang may hold on long enough to play a role that is a mixture of elder statesman, guardian of the armed forces, and wily politician.

While Yang himself may not last long, he may determine who among the younger generation gets a leg up at a crucial moment. A more pessimistic scenario suggests that intervention by Yang might help split an already fragmented armed forces. In such a vital power struggle, no one should assume that the armed forces are a single unit liable to support one leader at a time.

A younger clone of Yang Shangkun would be well placed to move up after Deng, but none exists. In fact, none of the younger leaders has sufficiently close relations with the armed forces to be assured of their support. All Chinese leaders know just how vital the military was in deciding the outcome of earlier struggles such as after Mao died or in 1989.

The closest there is to a man who might inspire confidence among conservative military men is Qiao Shi. Qiao was born in 1924 in Zhejiang Province and was a student organizer for the Party in Shanghai in the 1940s. He held various Party posts in the region but suffered badly during the Cultural Revolution. He re-emerged in the late 1970s in the central Party structure and headed the Party's Organisation Department for a little over a year from May 1984. He was appointed as Vice Premier in 1986 and as Politbureau member in 1987. He later became a member of the Politbureau's Standing Committee.

He is often described as 'shadowy', largely because he has worked so closely on internal Party issues and has effectively been in charge of public security. He reportedly declined to take the top Party job after the events of 1989, preferring to bide his time. Some speak of his closet liberal tendencies and yet others suggest that, like Yuri Andropov in the former Soviet Union, he is a nasty piece of work who wields power through his files on the equally nasty deeds of his rivals. Andropov was a transition figure to the short-lived Gorbachev era and Qiao may play a version of the Andropov role.

11

Longer Shots

IN the succession to Gorbachev there was a Yeltsin, but in China there is no such character on the horizon, with the possible exception of Zhao Ziyang. The massive decentralization of economic authority in China in recent years has meant that it may be pointless to look for a single successor to Deng. What we are seeing is the emergence of a more fragmented political system, with a major increase in power for China's regional leaders. As the economy grows more decentralized, regional leaders are less willing to surrender power and certainly money to the centre.

In the current age of uncertainty about the leadership in Beijing, they would be foolish to surrender too much of either to an unknowable future. Far better to sit tight and wait it out. As they wait, regional leaders grow accustomed to greater freedom and more difficult to persuade that any new leader is worthy of their active support. Power that has gravitated to the regions may not come back.

One man to watch may be the provincial leader of Guangdong, Xie Fei. Xie was born in 1932 in the province and has made his career there. As Guangdong's economy developed, so did Xie's clout and ability to rebuff Beijing. He was reportedly under repeated and powerful pressure to surrender his provincial power base and come to Beijing but felt that he was better served by staying far from the politics of the capital. He was elevated to the Politbureau in 1992 but has retained close ties to his regional power base. In a China with a weaker central government, the likes of Xie will find it opportune to spend more time away from the capital.

Other Politbureau leaders to watch in this category include Jiang Chunyun from Shandong, and Wu Bangguo from Shanghai. Tan Shaowen from Tianjin died soon after his appointment and serves as a reminder of the fragility of succession politics. These regional leaders are said to be reformers because they have supervised extensive reforms in their region. What is far less clear is their commitment to Beijing, whether or not the central government is ruled by like-minded reformers.

If the succession struggle is among the usual suspects, then the candidates are to be found among current leaders. If the struggle is more revolutionary, as was the case in Eastern Europe in 1989, then one might be looking for Havel-like figures among the dissidents. Chinese dissidents like to kid themselves by musing about analogies to Sun Yatsen who came back from abroad to rule parts of China after the end of the Qing dynasty. But those dissidents currently abroad have little organisation to support their cause and they snarl at each other too often to inspire confidence. None of the dissidents inside China is any more credible.

But there is one figure, to some extent similar to a Boris Yeltsin who came to power from being out of favour — Zhao Ziyang. The former Prime Minister and Party leader, who has strong regional support in Sichuan and southern China, was ousted by Deng in coalition with the conservatives in 1989. Zhao's disgrace has been mild and he has been spotted playing golf and talking to current leaders. Zhao is clearly biding his time, waiting for the succession to happen and for the verdict on the events of

1989 to be reversed. Zhao is not much older than Deng was when he returned from disgrace in the late 1970s to take power.

China has known plenty of reversed verdicts and although Zhao is far from an unqualified reformer his experience during and since 1989 may well have re-shaped his approach. Of course, vast sections of the armed forces will oppose his return, fearing that those who ousted Zhao in 1989 will, in turn, lose their jobs. If Zhao does return, splits in the armed forces are likely to be deep and dangerous.

Even if Zhao should succeed, the Chinese government he will inherit will be very different from the one he left in 1989. Central leaders simply lack much authority in a more fragmented and market-driven China. Zhao will not have enough clout in the regions to force them to surrender power or income. He certainly will not have much influence with the armed forces, especially if he settles scores from 1989. A far more realistic and effective scenario would be one in which China had a leader or better still a group of leaders who knew their limitations. China would thus operate as a looser collection of increasingly independent units. In a more informally federal China, look for an even more informal and flexible leadership.

2. Deng and the reform era

DENG Xiaoping was central to the reform process from the mid-1970s, when he first raised the possibilities of radical changes to the Maoist agenda for China. Though he was no original thinker and one of his great strengths was his ability to involve others, his role in the reform era was probably greater than any other single individual. His background in the politics of both the PRC and the CCP put him in a unique position to ensure the introduction of long planned and hoped for reforms.

Deng was seen as having been everywhere and done everything, and if not quite that, then at least as having been everywhere and done everything of importance in the development of the CCP. This position enabled him not only to be a main initiator of reform, but also to present himself and those actions as in defence of the CCP and communism. His death therefore faces the CCP with further problems of readjustment as it struggles to come to terms with the results of its own policies and its changing environment.

The situation to date

IN little over fifteen years from the end of 1978 to the middle of 1994, the PRC has moved from being regarded as a poorly organised command economy with a record of weak economic growth and political instability to a more politically stable, modernising society with high growth rates of about 10% of GNP per annum since 1978. It seems destined to become a major world economy. Deng Xiaoping was China's most prominent leader throughout the reform era, and it is inevitable that the achievements of those years should be associated with him personally. Deng was the architect of the reform era, but not the architect of reform.

The Politics of Counter Cultural Revolution

DENG Xiaoping retired from the last formal position he held in the party-state system in November 1989. Only in the period since, during the 1990s, has he developed a personality cult, becoming widely fêted as a one-man political movement and the centre of China's politics. The Third Plenary Session of the 11th Central Committee of the Chinese Communist Party which met in December 1978, and at which the decision was taken to abandon the earlier Mao-dominated policies of social change, is now regarded as the meeting that saw Deng's rise to power. Associated with this, Deng Xiaoping has also been held responsible for the reform era which followed and its later developments, as well as the sustained economic growth that has seen China become a major international economy.

Current politics necessarily mask the extent of Deng's personal involvement in the Third Plenum and the reform era. Equally, whatever future history may judge about the extent of Deng's personal involvement, he is undoubtedly more responsible than any other individual for the reform era that has come to bear his name. However, Deng and the events of 1978 and Deng and the reform era must be differentiated in a number of important ways if a balanced assessment is to be made of Deng Xiaoping's role in China's politics, and in particular the consequences of his death.

Deng Xiaoping's designation as the informal but none the less important 'paramount leader' or 'principal architect' dates not from 1978 but 1980 or 1982. Its precise origins and meaning are somewhat shrouded in mystery, but after Deng retired from daily administration in September 1985 he either became or remained the final level of decision-making. Well into the 1990s, for example, troops could still not be moved without Deng's authorization. Deng was given the title of 'paramount leader' after he refused appointment as Chairman of the CCP.

Deng's source of authority within the CCP came from his position in its history. He had been one of the youngest of the original revolutionary generation of the CCP and had grown up alongside its organisation. This put him in a central position of connections and relationships with almost all sections of the party's establishment. He had been recruited in France during the early 1920s by Zhou Enlai — whom Deng himself said he regarded as his 'elder brother'. He had studied in Moscow during a crucial period in the CCP's evolution and returned to China to serve in the party's central office. He became a peasant organiser in Southwest China during the late 1920s and early 1930s, and by 1933 had become allied with Mao Zedong's position in the party struggles of the time.

Deng was persecuted for his support of Mao in 1933, and a special relationship developed between the two that remained solid for over thirty years and significant well into the 1970s, even after the Cultural Revolution when Deng Xiaoping fell from grace. In particular during the Sino-Japanese War this relationship led to Deng becoming Mao's eyes and ears in the field of battle against the Japanese as political commissar of the 129th Division of the Eighth Route Army based in the Taihang Mountains.

These years of Deng's military service were of vital importance both in and after the mid-1950s when Deng became General Secretary of the CCP, and during the 1970s and the reform era when Deng was crucially able to rely on the support of the People's Liberation Army [PLA]. For much of the post-1949 period he was the army's favourite party cadre and the CCP's preferred military leader. In addition, a large part of Deng's later authority came from the paradox of his having been both close to Mao Zedong and a major victim of the Cultural Revolution.

One apparent reason that Deng was reluctant to be pushed into a senior position was his analysis of past political mistakes and his desire to see a more genuine collective leadership. However, that desire is easily exaggerated, particularly with his increasing age and impatience during the late 1980s. Though he may have started out as one amongst equals, that was certainly not how he ended up. On the contrary by the late 1980s the parallels with Mao's extreme personalisation of politics and in particular his poor treatment of his loyal lieutenants were becoming a little disturbing. Both Hu Yaobang (in 1987) and Zhao Ziyang (in 1989) fell from political grace when friction developed with Deng over the latter's personal authority, and he removed his patronage.

Earlier there had been a more distinct recognition that reform was a broad-based movement led by a coalition within the CCP's leadership. Throughout the 1970s Deng's greatest achievement was to build a coalition for China's future within the CCP. Right from his first recall to office in 1973 after disgrace and internal exile during the Cultural Revolution Deng became active in rallying those who believed that the politics of Cultural Revolution had to be rejected.

Through his military connections Deng was able to win over almost immediately those within the People's Liberation Army who wanted military modernisation. Through his party connections he was able to mobilise first former loyal Maoists, such as Chen Yun, and later former leaders persecuted by Mao, such as Bo Yibo, all of whom felt there was a desperate need for economic reform and were prepared to implement the policies they had designed and developed in both the mid-1950s and early 1960s when responsible for economic planning. Even when Deng fell from grace again under pressure from the 'Gang of Four' and more radical elements within the CCP, this group created a government-in-waiting content to bide its time.

Mao's death and the arrest of the 'Gang of Four' was the catalyst for their successful bid for power. Between Mao's death and March 1978, the composition of the CCP's leadership changed as dramatically as it had during 1966-8 and the Cultural Revolution. This time, however, the victors were those who had been removed in the Cultural Revolution and who had survived; and this time the leadership changed without the mass activity of the late 1960s. By the end of 1978 the CCP was ready to take the final moves in the Counter Cultural Revolution, rejecting its policies of economic and social change, and rehabilitating Mao's earlier protagonists.

The reform coalition's platform was fundamentally conservative. Their analysis was that if the CCP was to survive then it had to restore its traditions of popular support and emphasize economic modernisation rather than political correctness. Paradoxically then, what resulted was a policy of less government, particularly in economic management, allied with political messages reconstructing the history of the CCP. For the CCP, though less for the population in general, the reconstruction of the past was a central part of legitimising both their past and contemporary policies and behaviour.

The policy of less government is also important for understanding not only Deng's but also the CCP's role in the process of economic development during the reform era. The leadership of the CCP likes to claim responsibility for the results of reform. While it is clearly the case that the CCP created the conditions and set the parameters for economic modernisation, its role has declined as market forces and decentralized politics developed. There has been very little planning in the economic reform process, and its successes have often come because entrepreneurs have seen opportunities regardless of CCP or government action.

The state sector's share of economic activity has decreased dramatically during the era of reform, so that it is now confined to about a quarter of GDP. Growth has come in the collective, private and foreign-funded sectors of the economy. Though governments, especially local governments, play important roles in all these sectors, they rarely take initiatives. The lack of direct central government or CCP involvement in economic development is even the case for the most trumpeted of the CCP's reforms, such as the Special Economic Zones [SEZ].

Despite government involvement their growth and eventual success has been more the result of economic restructuring in the dynamic economies of East Asia which brought them to China in and after 1987. Difficult as it may now be to imagine, the initial policy of the CCP in establishing the SEZ was being judged a failure by the mid-1980s.

Something similar also applies to one of Deng Xiaoping's last and most famous policy initiatives. In the second half of 1989 the CCP created a self-induced recession by administrative means. By 1992 a substantial debate had emerged within the leadership about the speed at which reform should proceed. Deng took the initiative by travelling to the most economically advanced and export-oriented East and Southern regions on a well-publicised 'journey of inspection'. By giving his imprimatur to growth-oriented activities the 'Journey South' successfully changed national policy. However, all the evidence suggests that, while official policy may have changed with Deng's actions, economic activity had already long since picked up speed, and in ways outside the limits set by central government.

China in the World and Economic Reform

BY most standards the greatest domestic achievements of China under Deng Xiaoping were in the area of both economic modernisation and international relations, and the relationship between the two. When the CCP had come to power in 1949 one of its main platforms was the promise of economic modernisation. Almost thirty years later the CCP's record was considerably tarnished. Though there had been economic growth and even at times increased prosperity, particularly during the early 1950s, for some twenty or more years the economy had virtually stagnated.

For example, average wages had not increased from 1957 to 1977, and there had been occasions in between (as during the early 1960s in the wake of the disasters of the Great Leap Forward) when economic crises led once again to famine and starvation. At the same time, from the 1960s on, elsewhere in East Asia economies with many less obvious advantages were transforming themselves into 'tiger economies'.

By the early 1990s China was decreasingly seen as a 'backward' place. There has been considerable hyperbole about the size and speed of development of China's economy, with suggestions that it will be the largest aggregate economy in the world within twenty years. Perhaps even more remarkably, given the PRC's international reputation before 1978, economic growth has been achieved through foreign involvement in China's domestic economy, both by investment and a high degree of economic integration with the economies of East and Southeast Asia. Moreover, these changes in its international profile have clearly eased the CCP's way in international politics. International disapproval for the events of June 1989, when units of the PLA were sent into action against unarmed and peaceful demonstrators, has not led to the kind of action faced by a South Africa or Soviet Union during the 1970s and 1980s.

Any notion that either the CCP or Deng Xiaoping is totally responsible for all the consequences of the program of economic modernisation reflects a model of China's politics that disappeared in the 1980s as a result of reform, if indeed it ever existed. Totalitarianism stresses the centrality, omniscience and omnipotence of the state authority, in this case the Chinese Communist Party. Control has of course been a major concern for the CCP. At a relatively early stage in its deliberations on reform the leadership of the CCP determined that they would move to replace the central government's direct involvement in economic management with more indirect levers of macroeconomic control. However, the CCP leadership quite clearly has often been surprised by the degrees of freedom it has created, even allowing for the inadequacy of macroeconomic reform.

As already noted, one area in which the CCP has played a leading role and to great effect has been in the setting of the initial agenda and the framework for economic reform. Deng's role in that process was crucial: he harried and cajoled in order to ensure that policy instruments were developed and that policy implementation had some chance of success. It was not a totally thankless task, particularly given Deng's personal legitimacy from half a century of working at the centre of CCP politics and his earlier reputation as Mao's right-hand man.

It was an agenda that had its roots in earlier debates within the CCP and not simply the rejection of Mao's more idealistic notions. Greater decentralization in economic management, slower economic growth on a sound agricultural base, and a recognition of the importance of market forces provided the basis of the Second Five Year Plan devised under Chen Yun's direction in 1956. It was a plan effectively aborted by Mao Zedong's impatience during the Great Leap Forward. However, the economic crises of the early 1960s saw a return to these policies, and to the same policy makers. Though they were variously persecuted or side-lined again during the Cultural Revolution, by the end of the 1970s these same planners were ready with fresh ideas for China's economic future.

The key economic reforms were more far-reaching than simply the introduction of market forces into a command economy. Following the obvious example of its East Asian neighbours China embarked on an export-led growth strategy. In addition the state economy has undergone fundamental structural reform: the rural collective economy was basically to be dismantled; local government was to disengage itself from enterprise management; and decentralization was to be a guiding principle in both government and economic management.

Perhaps most remarkable of all, by 1994 the state sector of the economy accounted for only about half of all industrial output, the collective, private and foreign-related sectors having grown substantially in the interim. Two early reforms that signalled the discontinuity with the recent past were rural decollectivisation and the establishment of the Special Economic Zones [SEZ]. In the early 1960s and at a time of severe economic crisis those who were later to become the post-Mao reformers had first proposed the 'household responsibility system' as a way of encouraging rural initiative in the wake of the failure of the Great Leap Forward and not least in order to meet the massive shortfall in food production. Though it was obviously popular it soon fell foul of Mao's collectivist vision for China. After Mao's death and even before the Third Plenum, which approved the re-introduction of individual household production, a number of local leaders had experimented with similar systems in order to increase rural productivity. Within two years the rural sector was decollectivised and the boom in the agricultural economy provided the basis for further economic reform.

Unlike many of the initiatives of the reform era, policy on the Special Economic Zones is one area where Deng Xiaoping has claimed specific and public responsibility. The first SEZ was established shortly after the Third Plenum in order to attract foreign investment and technology. At first and well into the mid-1980s the SEZs were not wildly successful. Deng Xiaoping took the lead in persevering with their maintenance and, though both he and the CCP would undoubtedly wish to claim direct responsibility for their subsequent success, the causes are more complicated. In the mid-1980s a number of the 'tiger' economies of East Asia — notably Hong Kong and Taiwan — were under pressure to restructure. Driven by

high factor costs in their own economies enterprises de-
camped, often more or less intact, into China.

The Social Impact of Reform

DENG'S analysis of China's past ills led him to
advocate the replacement of direct controls by
indirect not just in the realms of economic reform, but
generally. Change can clearly be exaggerated, not least
because China remains a Communist Party State and
almost regardless of its ruling party a fundamentally pre-
modern state and society. Nonetheless, economic modernisation and the limited political reform permitted by
the CCP has wrought considerable social change. Perhaps
the most important of these were the redefinition of
politics that took place at the beginning of the reform era
and the consequent emergence of complex society. In turn
these developments have caused the CCP to reconsider its
processes of social control.

Before 1978 and during the Mao-dominated era of
China's politics, everything was regarded as politics, or
rather nothing was regarded as being apart from politics:
in the slogan of the Cultural Revolution, 'Politics was in
command'. The result was a fundamental social and
political paralysis. The CCP as the central locus of political
power was regarded as responsible for everything and as
a result little was done without its approval. Indeed, such
over-concentration of power rapidly became dysfunc-
tional since the CCP as an organisation became over-
loaded and could carry out neither its own functions nor
those of other institutions whose functions it was part

usurping and part being forced to replace through some kind of deference.

Deng's basic reform — the replacement of politics in command by economics— has changed power relations not only within the state but also within society. While it remains true that the old structures of the party-state remain powerful, they no longer monopolise everything, and there is no longer a single hierarchy of social, political and economic acceptability. Independent entrepreneurs can become economically wealthy and socially important in their own locality, and these days it is even possible that the local party will come and pay court rather than the other way around. In the media and amongst intellectuals this redefinition of politics has been particularly important. It has not only allowed greater degrees of freedom within activities, and even a degree of apoliticalness, but necessarily the media and other devices are the carriage of ideas and values, not all of which may be immediately acceptable to the CCP. The 1980s saw a publication expansion and revolution in China — of books, magazines and newspapers — for the most part limited only by supplies of paper.

The redefinition of politics was something that by all accounts had preoccupied Deng during his internal exile at the time of the Cultural Revolution. According to various reports he had spent much time walking round his courtyard considering where the momentum of modernisation had been lost and how it could be restored. Deng had become concerned that the CCP's legitimacy had been badly tarnished and that nothing but economic growth and reform — which would necessarily go hand in hand — could restore the fortunes of both the CCP and the PRC. He blamed, specifically, the lack of democracy, political uncertainty and instability, and the behaviour of cadres whose only motivation seemed to be the pursuit of personal power and privilege. Solutions were sought in an appeal to democracy; recognition and acceptance of partial interests, in both economics and politics; an emphasis on rules and regulations; and attempts to ensure the abilities and virtue of officials.

The recognition of partial and even private interests is perhaps the most tangible evidence of redefined politics for a CCP which previously brooked no qualification to its monopoly of political power. In the new policies of the 1980s, while the prospect of overall economic growth is held out to the population as a whole, the individual is positively encouraged to take the initiative and responsibility in order to amass personal wealth. However, the political consequences of the CCP no longer claiming omnipotence or omniscience are equally as important since it now, albeit in a limited way, encourages the articulation of interests outside its control, as for example demands for better working conditions or higher social status.

In the 1980s the democratic and legal forms that had previously been deliberately subordinated to the CCP's political control were revitalised at Deng's urging. The redefinition of politics did not provide an independent judiciary or a total separation of party and state, but it did begin to provide a large measure of regularisation that had earlier been missing. Civil and criminal codes were passed, greater distinction between the executive and representative functions of government work were made and given organisational form. It became respectable again, and even desirable, to be a lawyer; and regular general elections — direct elections to county level people's governments — have been held since 1979.

The redefinition of politics has also been directed at improving the performance of officials. In 1980 Deng delivered a trenchant critique of their more obvious pathological behaviour: the excessive personal and institutional concentration of authority, the lifelong tenure of leadership and various abuses of privilege. The greater distinction between party and government activity that has followed during the 1980s assisted in combatting the over-concentration of political power. However, more significant has been a set of policies designed to ensure that the leading cadres of the 1990s are younger, better educated and more specialised than their predecessors.

These policies were implemented with a great deal of success in a relatively short period of time. The average age of provincial leaders and ministers dropped considerably in the second half of the 1980s, and most are now college graduates, whereas even ten years ago it was common to find few with any formal education beyond the most rudimentary. However, the real impact of such reforms is harder to gauge. As with the introduction of laws and regulations and other structural changes, the test is in the manner of their operation, and a new political culture undoubtedly takes time to emerge.

The redefinition of politics, and by extension other spheres of social and economic life, was an integral part of the reform process. It was designed to ensure stability and sustained economic modernisation, as well as to restore the legitimacy of the CCP. However, it does not automatically follow that the CCP has been able to manage the process of redefining politics exactly as it would like. The CCP had no blueprint for reform, and some of the developments of the 1980s were clearly unforeseen either in kind or degree. The most obvious example was the popular demonstrations in Beijing during April, May and June of 1989 when the CCP leadership was clearly unsure how to react. Less dramatic but potentially more serious for the future were the scale of economic regionalism that has emerged with reform and the growth of China's new rich.

The CCP's response to its self-induced problems of social control has been an appeal to 'Chineseness' as a unifying and mobilisatory political myth, rather than to the class conflict that characterised the Mao-dominated years of China's politics. This pre-modern form of nationalism is more vaguely cultural than one allied to a specific state or government. Though the CCP attempts to portray itself as the guardian of this 'Chineseness' it is almost as if it also sub-consciously realises that the political system is in transition. Even within the CCP there is a recognition that the definition of 'Chineseness' may lie outside its control: hence its importance as a current political issue.

Transformations in the Chinese State

IT is common to regard China's reform era as one that has delivered economic reform and growth, but one in which substantial political change has not been permitted. Deng has often been equated with Lee Kuan Yew and presented as arguing that economic modernisation can and should occur without political change.

However, there have been not only significant political reforms, but also the start of substantial transformations in the Chinese state. As already noted, the redefinition of politics has yielded political space for private activities, and not only in the exercise of economic entrepreneurship. The changing structure of China's economy, and in particular the growth of new corporate entities, has started to influence its political economy and the basis of state power. The growth of an intense regionalism presents a challenge not for the most part to the unity of the state but to the relationship between central government and the provinces.

The growth of the private sector of the economy has generated much interest, both inside and outside China, not least because of the contrast with the recent past. However, it has not as yet seen the growth of an independent capitalist class who might come to challenge for state power. The private sector has for the most part been small-scale and low-technology. Large parts of the retail sector and many commercial activities have become dominated by private entrepreneurs, but the private sector's share of industrialisation remains small. When private enterprise wants to grow the tendency is for it to cease activity in the private sector and to restructure itself as a collective sector enterprise.

The collective sector represents not only the most dynamic sector of the industrial economy, but also the growth of China's new corporate sector. Before the reform era the collective sector was that part of the public economy not governed by the state plan — collective sector enterprises received no automatic or subsidised allocations. It was essentially a second and poorer state sector. One ideological justification for this difference was that while state enterprises belonged to all the people, collective enterprises belonged to the responsible collective: either a locality or the workers in the enterprise themselves.

With reform the collective sector has been more able to respond to market pressures and structural reforms. State enterprises have larger overheads, including guaranteed labour costs, that collective enterprises do not face. Enterprise reform started mainly in the countryside with town and village collectives being encouraged to take advantage of the new economic environment. Underutilised resources were turned to more productive ends — agricultural machinery repair workshops in the suburban villages became light industrial factories manufacturing for export; car pools became taxi services, lorry teams freight delivery services. By the mid-1990s there were many suburban villages in South and East China that had become growing industrial conglomerates with little or no relationship to agricultural production.

Increasingly too after 1984, as the processes of economic reform were also brought to urban China, the same principles of enterprise reform were applied. However, in this case many state sector enterprises, or even social organisations with some economic capacity — such as schools or trade unions — were able to redirect their under-utilised resources in the establishment of collective sector enterprises. A steel factory with a glass products workshop might establish a glass bottle and jamjar factory as a collective enterprise; a machine workshop might become an electronic timer factory. Often where the new collectives came out of state enterprises the latter would establish a holding company. Almost always local government would be involved in the new collective enterprise, through the provision of some equity (usually land and buildings) and administrative regulation. The new collective sector has some claim to be regarded as a local government economy because of the extent of these relationships.

The strength of the local government economy helps explain the third way in which the collective sector has grown. Private entrepreneurs wanting to grow and become more technologically advanced or capital intensive usually turn their enterprise into a collective in cooperation with local government. The latter provides not only some equity and political protection but also a better economic environment. Collective enterprises can more easily obtain loans for development and at lower rates of interest than the private sector. They also pay less taxes and fees and are subject to less administrative regulation.

The growth of the collective sector is likely gradually to alter the political economy of CCP rule, and indeed at the local level is already doing so. Local government, business people, local entrepreneurs and enterprise managers still come together under the aegis of the CCP, but with new agendas. Party meetings are more like a cross between a club for local notables and the Rotary or Lions associations.

At the more rarefied end of the political hierarchy regionalism is also having an important impact on the exercise of politics. China has rarely been as centralised or conformist as the totalitarian image would suggest. Since the late 1930s the CCP has adopted an administrative policy of 'doing the best according to local conditions' in which the centre laid down broad guidelines while detailed policies on implementation were a matter for local determination. Even during the height of a Soviet-style political economy in China during the early 1950s there was considerably more decentralization in economic management permitted than was the case in the Soviet Union.

None the less, through its policies of decentralization in economic management, the introduction of market forces and of increased external economic relations ('the open door'), the reform era has markedly shifted the balance of power between central and provincial governments. For various reasons, and with the exception of the two predominantly non-Han Chinese areas of Tibet and Xinjiang, the intense regionalism is unlikely to lead to the 'break-up' of the Chinese polity in the way that political disintegration came to characterise the implosion of communism in Eastern Europe and the former Soviet Union. However, it is likely to lead to and has already demonstrated the ability for regions and provinces to be significantly more autonomous.

The consequences of these increased powers of self-governance are, as might be expected given the size and variety of China, different from region to region and province to province. In Guangdong, the leading southern province and the first to experience full-scale reform, self-governance means a relative economic independence where the province keeps a large part of its own revenue but as a corollary takes almost no capital investment from Beijing. The CCP for its part is becoming sidelined as an institution. Its senior leaders may be members of the CCP, but their effective base of operations is now in the provincial government.

Shanxi Province in contrast is a long-time centre of heavy industry and a northern province with deep CCP roots since the Sino-Japanese War. Here there are almost opposite trends in both economics and politics. The province is a vast coalfield and has required close relations with Beijing for investment not only in its domestic industrial development but also in the development of coal transportation facilities with the rest of the country. In Shanxi's politics leadership positions in the provincial government are reserved for the superannuated. The CCP not only remains powerful as an organisation, it is also quite clearly an organisation transforming itself, not least by taking Shanxi province as its explicit primary focus. In addition, it has deliberately adopted a more populist profile, and set itself both modern (infrastructural) and post-modern (quality of life) agendas.

Problems and challenges

THE experience of modernisation elsewhere in the world and elsewhen in history has been that social dislocation and political change are necessary consequences. The key questions are not whether there will be difficulties but of what kind and with what consequences. In China's case the rapid pace of change and high economic growth rates since 1978 have probably magnified many of the problems that have resulted. In particular, the transition from a command towards a market economy, and the movement of large numbers of economic migrants within the country, both within a relatively short period of time, have created additional strains. At the same time and by the same token, China's experience of problems in the present and immediate future does not of itself indicate an end to political stability or the disintegration of an ordered society.

Political difficulties

POLITICAL change during the reform era may well have been more fundamental and far-reaching than either the CCP or conventional wisdom would yet care to admit. None the less it has not occurred without its problems and paradoxes. Perhaps the most startling is the extent to which China remains a pre-modern political system. The very fact that the death of Deng Xiaoping should give so much room for thought about the future of the PRC and the capacity for survival of the CCP is proof enough of that. It was Deng's political persona which was seen to drive the reform process for much of the time since 1978 just as it has been Deng's personal authority that served as the guarantee to the more conservative-minded that change has remained minimal and will continue to be so.

A major paradox of the reform era centres around Deng's personal role in the reform process. One of the key political reforms initiated by Deng Xiaoping as early as January 1980 has been the attempt to institutionalise politics — to remove the personalist characteristics that exemplified the Mao-dominated era of China's politics. To that end Deng stressed not the role of individuals but of collective leadership, 'party life' and the importance of regulation.

On the other hand, much of the reform momentum, particularly after the mid-1980s, would not have been maintained without Deng's personal intervention. Throughout the 1980s he intervened in politics consistently to check political liberalisation and to ensure the maintenance of relatively fast economic reform. The most spectacular example of the latter was Deng's 'Inspection Tour of the South' which virtually single-handedly reignited intra-leadership enthusiasm for fast export-oriented growth after the government-induced recession during the second half of 1989.

One reason that Deng may have felt it necessary to intervene personally even after he had withdrawn from the 'front line' of administration after the mid-1980s was because there were genuine political disagreements within the leadership. In the early stages of reform the leadership could unite relatively easily on what it did not want (the

Cultural Revolution) and how to proceed (gradually with the rural areas as the base). However, differences began to appear in the leadership with the introduction of reform to urban China in late 1984. By the National Party Conference of September 1985 these had become quite obvious and well-articulated. This was not a dispute about whether there should be reform, but a series of differences of opinion about the speed and general direction of reform.

Disagreement within the leadership of the CCP has resulted largely from the process of China's modernisation. It is easy to equate China's post-1978 economic growth with the modernisation of Taiwan, Hong Kong, Singapore and South Korea in and after the 1960s. While there are many points of similarity there are also significant differences, including in particular that China's post-1978 growth and development relied to some extent on earlier phases of modernisation. Overall the economy grew at an annual average rate of 6% of GNP, despite major disasters and recessions during those years. A modern bureaucracy and education system were established from the early 1950s. The period since 1978 has seen economic restructuring not first-stage modernisation. One important political consequence is that China now possesses two modernising élites who may often conflict: those from before 1978 and the era of Mao-dominated politics; and those closely associated with the reform agenda.

China also differs from other modernising régimes of East Asia because it is so much bigger and so much more varied. The centralised modernising strategies of a Taiwan, South Korea or even a Japan were not readily available. Decentralization was and remains a *sine qua non* for economic growth. And decentralization has generally strengthened the hand of the provinces vis-à-vis central government and led to even greater diversity and disagreement within the leadership.

However, that trend has not necessarily meant that every province has aspired to less central involvement, or even that each has favoured faster reform in national debates about that topic. Some provinces — Guangdong is the obvious example — clearly have sought greater autonomy, less involvement with the centre and a fairly rapid sustained reform process. At the same time, there is a wide variety of attitudes to be found on the speed of reform ranging from the cautious to the enthusiastic. There are even provinces which, while favouring reform, have preferred to lobby for greater central investment and involvement, sometimes even quite aggressively. Xinjiang, for example, made this point forcefully when it engaged in protectionist measures during 1989 and 1990 because, in its own view, if it was not to receive central assistance then it had to look after its own activities.

Considerations of the élite apart, the problem for the CCP in initiating reform of any kind, but particularly political reform, is that it allows itself almost no room for manoeuvre and must necessarily create a revolution of rising expectations, which it can only meet with more fundamental reform. To date the CCP has only demonstrated that it wants to reform the system it has created but still retain monopoly control: to give in to external demands but still to control the extent to which it meets those demands and their results.

Nowhere was this problem clearer than in the CCP's

appeal to democracy, not least because that term had no precise meaning when reform started. At the time of the Third Plenum the CCP leadership, even including Deng Xiaoping, was prepared to talk of democracy as almost the unfettered will of the people. However, within a few months as debate became wide-ranging and possibly CCP-threatening, then the appeal to democracy became an appeal to 'socialist democracy', designed to improve the operation of the party-state system, certainly not to replace it.

A similar problem of rising democratic expectations became acute once again in the late 1980s. Through that decade intellectuals were encouraged, both directly and indirectly, to participate in politics. However, some began trying to move reform farther and faster than many of the CCP's senior leaders were prepared to countenance, and by the end of 1988 — even before the street demonstrations of April and May brought matters to a head — it was clear that conflict was on the way.

As the 1990s move on, it would not be surprising to find the emergence of yet new voices from within the political and economic structures being created by the reform process claiming a slice of the political action. Sometimes, as in the case of the development of the collective sector of the economy to date, those new voices may have very close connections to the established party-state. However, it is the CCP's ability to assimilate interests, maintain its own equilibrium and initiate further reform that will be the key to its future.

Economic development

THE consequences and problems of rapid economic development in China since the late 1970s have been so obvious and so potentially threatening that it is often difficult to imagine growth being sustained. Despite the very real achievements of reform, China is still saddled with a large and extremely inefficient state sector.

At the same time the relatively rapid move from a command economy towards a market economy has highlighted some old problems and created new ones. China lacks an adequate economic infrastructure, both physical and financial, and the consequences of reform include inflation, corruption and massive dislocation. While these and other problems cannot be dismissed, even more serious difficulties for the maintenance of both reform and economic growth may be found with the inadequacies of the workforce and the scale of environmental degradation.

Despite the excitement generated by the growth of the private, collective and foreign-funded sectors of the economy, the state sector remains of considerable socio-economic importance and may well be a significant check on further economic growth. The state sector dominates the heavy industrial sector and produces roughly half of all industrial output. During the reform era the proportion of the workforce in the state sector has even increased marginally from 16.8% to 18.2%. Because it is the tangible manifestation of state socialism it has been and remains largely inefficient in economic terms. Its equipment and processes are usually old-fashioned and in poor working order. Its labour costs are high, not least because state

Deng Xiaoping in France, 1921.

Deng Xiaoping, Liu Bocheng and families, Wu'an, Hebei, 1945.

Deng Xiaoping and Zhuo Lin, Taihang Base Area, shortly after their marriage, 1939.

Deng Xiaoping and Mao Zedong, Beijing, 1962.

Deng Xiaoping and Ho Chi Minh at Beijing Airport, 1965.

Deng Xiaoping and Zhou Enlai, Beijing, 1963.

Deng Xiaoping in Zhongshan County, Guangdong, 1984.

High rise, Sanya, Hanan, South China, 1994, (left).

Low rise, Zuo Quan, Shanxi, North China, 1994, (below).

Bar and amusement arcade, Taiyuan, 1994.

Stock exchange news, Hangzhou, 1992.

Chinese restaurant for the new rich, Hangzhou, 1993.

sector enterprises have been the social base for the unions afforded a special place in CCP ideology.

Reform of the state sector has not proved as easy as the CCP appeared at one time to expect. There have been significant advances. The change in industrial development strategy during 1979-1982, which moved resources from heavy industry and prepared for the emergence of a market-driven consumer industry, highlights an important difference from the experience of other state socialist systems in reform. Some state sector enterprises and even former government departments and branch agencies have been commercialised. The appropriation of the assets of state enterprises by their newly-established subordinate collective enterprises marks the distinct impact of market forces on the state sector.

However, economic inefficiencies remain and are a fundamental feature of the state sector. There is still resistance to the operation of market forces in state sector activities — such as the employment of labour — and fears of what may happen if the state ceased to underwrite the economic operation and social welfare provisions of state sector enterprises. Some state enterprises have been sold off, but there are many which are kept going though technically bankrupt.

Transport difficulties similarly pre-date the reform era. North-south transportation of people and freight has been historically difficult and was but little improved after 1949. The main river systems — the Yangtze and the Yellow River — flow west-east, and there are relatively few railroads (for the population and distances covered). Until the 1980s there were almost no long-distance roads or road-haulage, and a similarly under-developed domestic air-system. China has one of the world's largest coalfields in the Ordos Basin of North China, but because of domestic transport problems South China imports coal from the rest of the world.

Air transport can be rapidly developed but it is very expensive, particularly for freight. In China's case the urgency of the situation has simply resulted in operations based on unreliable equipment and poorly-trained staff. China's appalling safety record in air transport is the most obvious manifestation of a wholly inadequate operation attempting to grow rapidly.

An important explanation of China's transport and other economic problems lies with the 1960s and early 1970s policy of directing most capital investment to the development of the relatively isolated Central-West and Southwest. Mao Zedong believed that the country should be able to defend itself by retreating into the isolated areas in case of attack. The result was that the more economically advanced areas were starved of resources. At the same time extremely inefficient and unproductive enterprises and industries were being developed in the more isolated areas. Spiralling unit costs for production met poor communications, weak supplies, and almost non-existent markets.

The dismantling of the command economy changed all this and allowed some of the earlier imbalances to be redressed. However, other social and economic problems have resulted precisely from the process of change itself. Corruption is probably the most obvious of those. Reform has redistributed the economic capital of the state sector, though not always in ways which are strictly legal or even acceptable. Previously under-used machinery or equipment, for example, may be appropriated with no intention of payment ever being effected. There is a ready justification: state property belongs to 'The People' and this redistribution is simply 'The People' reasserting their property rights.

The development of a quasi-private sector alongside a public economy has permitted undoubtedly corrupt as well as simply suspect practices to emerge in the relationship between the two. For example, goods can be purchased in the state sector at a cheap subsidised price but sold at the higher market value in the free economy. For a state sector manager with access to state subsidised goods in short supply and faced by an unproductive and inefficient state enterprise, the pressures to speculate in such ways must be considerable for both economic and political reasons.

Even more startling, the relationships between the state planned economy and the free market may allow essentially private enterprises to establish themselves within the protection and benefits of the state sector. One particularly profitable 'entertainment complex' in East China even managed through its personal contacts to establish itself in cooperation with a trade union organisation as a tax-exempt charity.

At the same time the speed and pressure for change, even government policy that emphasises the use of individual initiative, all encourage the search for short cuts and instant results. Bribery is common for business people who need not only to get around in the system in some way but simply to ensure economically reliable results in a still largely unregulated market.

Large-scale fraud and embezzlement have also been

fairly common occurrences in the reform era. The New China News Agency reported a record 50,000 prosecuted cases of economic crime in 1993. Nearly half of them each involved more than 10,000 yuan RMB. Many of those prosecuted were officials of the state, including one vice minister, 46 departmental and 848 county level officials. Crimes range from the sale of official car number plates to major instances of bribery, embezzlement and fraud. In the first half of 1993, there were 95 reported cases involving more than one million yuan RMB each. The largest was the embezzlement of 30.44 million yuan RMB by a group of accountants in a Hainan bank.

Inflation, too, is largely a consequence of the gap between the command and market economies and the need to bring the two together as quickly as possible. In the past the inequity between urban and rural prices was a major and increasing source of tension throughout the 1980s and into the 1990s. Removing that inequity — which effectively meant that rural areas heavily subsidised the towns and cities — has had an inflationary impact and caused social dislocation.

The run on banks and savings accounts in urban areas during the middle of 1988 has had shock effects which continue to be felt and remembered by both government and the population at large. A central problem in the control of inflation is central government's inability to put a system of macro-economic controls in place. The replacement of administrative controls with macro-economic instruments for national economic management has long been planned but remains stymied at the design stage. Central government has had to rely on the tried and tested administrative methods to control inflation. Each time it threatens to run away the situation has been stabilised through crude administrative intervention rather than any more sophisticated controls of money supply or interest rates.

Beyond the establishment of the People's Bank of China as the central bank few macro-economic controls have been introduced. This is symptomatic of the lack of an adequate national financial infrastructure which in turn presents limits to the growth of an integrated domestic market. There are clearly still substantial limits to the emergence of a nationally integrated economy. From the available evidence it seems that inter-provincial trade has barely increased during the reform era; growth has come from international trade in exports and imports.

Transportation, corruption and the lack of an adequate financial infrastructure are all high-profile and immediate problems. In the longer-term the inadequate provision of education and training, and lack of attention to policies for sustainable development may cause severe limits to continued economic development. Expenditure on education has barely risen during the reform era. There have been considerable increases in the provision of educational services at the most advanced end of the university system. However, there have been few if any improvements at the levels of skilled and semi-skilled labour. This must necessarily act as a brake as there is a limit to the growth that can be predicated on unskilled migrant (from poorer parts of the country) labour working shift-work on low-technology assembly lines — very much the norm up to now.

The visitor to Beijing now compared to the late 1970s would notice that the skies are no longer clear through the winter, but yellowed with pollution. Every North China city is thick with coal dust, particularly during winter. Rivers and waterways have similarly become repositories for industrial effluent and waste. These are serious problems and limits to economic growth but still not as immediate as the overuse of natural resources, particularly water, in some areas. North China has had severe water shortages for the last few years because of poor environmental controls and management. Drought is historically fairly common and this, combined with no environmental protection, has reduced or poisoned water tables in many places. The Fen River, which ran through Taiyuan (the capital of Shanxi Province), was a very broad flowing river until as late as the mid-1970s: now it barely exists. It is common to find industrial enterprises on three-day working weeks because of water shortages, even in the state sector and even in strategic industries. Residential areas are even more rationed.

There is at least one independent (of government) environmental watch-dog agency in China, that established by the former journalist Dai Qing in Beijing. There is also environmental protection legislation in some of the provinces, and some provincial leaders have made policy stands on the need for environmental protection, sustainable development and 'green' policies. However, the major problem facing all such activities is that there is no generalised acceptance of such regulation, and probably not much recognition of regulation as a whole.

Social outlook

THE social impact of reform has been both great and problematical, though not always in the ways articulated by the leaders of the CCP. Their primary concern has been to ensure the necessary measure of support for the CCP as China changes. This explains their appeal, as already noted, to a kind of pre-modern nationalism — an undefined 'Chineseness' — instead of earlier selfless and collectivist ideals. None the less, the need to take account of value change is by no means trivial. People's lives are changing dramatically, well within single lifetimes. New lifestyles are to be explored and new social contracts to be negotiated. The peasant girl from Inner Mongolia can now become a factory worker in Hangzhou. The process worker in Wuhan may now have to provide for his own health insurance and pension scheme.

The potential for the emergence of feelings of positive self-development and of resentment probably exist in equal measure. The social impact of corruption is probably even more important than its economic effects. The CCP may be concerned with what it sees as 'moral decay' because it cannot cope with the uncertainty of an open society. However, it is also the case that corruption is likely to undermine the authority of the CCP, and an excess challenges social cohesion. In the ten years up to 1992, China recorded 2,247,900 cases of corruption. More than 1.8 million CCP members and cadres were punished, of which 745 were cadres at the provincial level, 7,890 at the prefectural level, and 56,474 at the county level. 188,100 members of the CCP were expelled for corruption during this period.

The CCP argues that corruption results from a largely individual moral failure. However, corruption may also be seen as a necessary result of China's current stage of development. There is no rule of law or indeed a general acceptance of regulation. This means that corruption is actually difficult to define as an activity, and largely a temporary phenomenon, set to reduce as economic actors impose regulation in their own self-interest. Corruption occurs because in part individuals are being encouraged to take initiatives but the regulatory frameworks within which they operate are weak or non-existent. The CCP in consequence has to try to instil some wider responsibility by stressing the results of moral decay.

The lack of regulative frameworks creates enormous social problems. China has never been able to provide free social welfare to much more than about 19% of its population. Now that figure has shrunk to about 7% and not even then everyone working in the state sector is covered. Social welfare provision in the new enterprises has until very recently been virtually non-existent and remains extremely poor.

One of the reasons for the growth of the collective sector has been precisely lack of labour regulation, lower labour costs and greater flexibility. New entrepreneurs in the faster growing areas can and do recruit teenagers from the poorer parts of the country to come and work for low wages relative to the standard of the faster growing areas but high relative to their own home-town standards. There is usually little if any provision for worker's insurance or pension schemes, though most employers provide accommodation. It is fairly typical to hear employers say that their workforce requires neither a pension nor health insurance because they are young, in good health and not near retirement age. In practice a sick worker is simply dropped from the workforce.

Those who travel for guaranteed employment in the factories and enterprises of the faster growing areas face and may cause considerable social problems, including those associated with acceptance by their host communities. It is common to see teenagers from the inland and poorer western provinces in factories, workshops and enterprises all over East and South China. Often they are from poor peasant backgrounds and are despised by the richer Easterners who look down on assembly line and factory employment as 'dirty work' fit only for migrant workers. There is little integration and many rapidly become homesick. However, the option to return to one's native place may be limited as it is usual that the young worker has agreed to pay the recruiting agent a fee, often a percentage of the first year's wages.

The problems of recruited workers pale into insignificance by comparison with those associated with the estimated 50-100 million 'drifters' who move, largely from economic necessity, looking for work. These migrants are to be found all over China and not only in the faster growing parts of the country. The easing of restrictions on movement, the introduction of market forces into the economy, and the emphasis on individual effort have led many to look for work elsewhere. Large numbers have drifted to Guangdong, Shanghai and the Eastern seaboard. There has also been significant migration of this kind — involving peddlers, small business people, shopkeepers and the like — into other parts of China.

Such migration undoubtedly causes problems but for the most part it is unlikely to have any longer-term adverse significance for social harmony. Tibet is an obvious exception, where Han Chinese migrants have threatened local culture by moving into previously Tibetan residential areas and economic activities.

A defining feature of reform has been a dramatic change in the urban landscape. Central business districts in most large cities and towns have been physically transformed. Ranks of skyscrapers have replaced low density administrative blocks. Traffic schemes have become more complex, streetscapes more commercial. Most cities and towns have expanded their areas of economic activity — even if official government boundaries have not yet been adjusted to take account of such growth. Many former suburban villages in East and South China have become largely satellite towns, based on industrial production and fused into the conurbation.

These villages were the first areas to be allowed to experiment with new industrial enterprises and other economic activities. They have been at the heart of economic growth, particularly in the collective sector. As they have grown they have merged in a number of ways into the urban area — including the ownership, control or management of land within the towns and cities — while still retaining their official 'rural' registration. The advantages of such arrangements are many, not least because rural China has a more flexible economic environment for enterprise development. Urbanisation of this kind presents no problem in itself, though there is clearly an additional strain on urban public services.

However, the existence of two or more regulative

frameworks for otherwise identical activities or environments may be a source of tension and dysfunctionality. Where one urban plot may not be developed for residential or hotel use simply because it is classified as the responsibility of an urban district, but its neighbour can because it belongs to a suburban village, there is potential for considerable resentment.

Population control has been a relative success of the reform era. At least in urban China the spectre of rapid over-population has diminished. However, paradoxically, the success of the population control policy has the potential to cause problems. Particularly in urban areas the 'one child' policy has led younger generations to have radically different expectations from those held earlier by their parents. The much discussed phenomenon of 'little emperors and empresses' is the result of doting parents and grandparents who spoil their single off-spring.

Already it is clear that there is a significant generation gap between those who grew to maturity before 1976 (and the death of Mao Zedong) and later generations. Despite the widespread unpopularity of the politics and policies of the Cultural Revolution, earlier generations seem generally more altruistically-minded. New entrepreneurs from those earlier generations are more likely than their generational successors to engage in acts of public philanthropy, such as endowing a school or building with a ceremonial arch. The impact of a generation of single children may cause not simply generational conflict but also a paradigm shift in urban China's world-view.

The future

THE enormity of the challenges China faces suggests an uneasy future. Though economic collapse and political chaos are unlikely, they cannot be dismissed as of no concern. Rapid events in and after 1989 in the Soviet Union and Eastern Europe seem to offer two instructive lessons to the understanding of China without Deng Xiaoping.

The first is to question the prospects for both national unity and the continued position of the CCP. The second is more generally to underline the difficulties of prediction—most commentators were taken aback by the scale and speed of imploding communism. However, the longer-term processes of change already underway in China, and the contrast to other historical examples—the experience of the Soviet Union and Eastern Europe, as well as the evolution of authoritarian capitalism in East Asia — suggest that prediction may be on surer ground.

Political disintegration along the lines of the Soviet Union or Yugoslavia is generally unlikely. However, China is already characterised by a high degree of regionalism that has dramatically altered the workings of its political system and is coming to influence domestic political style. National unity may not be in question but China is becoming increasingly polycentrist. Though this is clearly neither political disintegration nor imploding communism, it is also likely to result in even more highly localised politics, and as part of that process the CCP too is becoming localised.

The CCP has mortgaged its future on the ability to

deliver economic growth and China's modernisation. However, continued economic growth depends on decentralization, the absence of central control and a lack of CCP interference — both nationally and locally. The future political system will build on the resources and linkages of the CCP and the party-state.

It may even emerge with no change of names or cries of revolution, and maintain the political myths and traditions of the PRC since 1949. However, CCP or no, China is almost certain to be a more diverse and loosely-bound political union.

Long-term Prospects

THE experience of the Soviet Union and Eastern Europe appears to present severe challenges to China's political future. However, it is far from clear that the parallels between China and the former Soviet Union are exact enough to justify predictions of either the implosion of communist rule or the disintegration of the unified state. Although the political structures of the PRC were established by and along the lines of the Soviet Union during the early 1950s, there the parallels end. The population of the USSR was more urbanised, intellectualised and more used to mass politics. Unlike its Soviet counterpart the CCP came to power through a protracted process of war and civil war, based on mass mobilisation. While that contrast does not guarantee the CCP wide popular support, it does provide the opportunity, particularly in North China, where its roots run deep.

Moreover, China's contemporary political culture differs in two important respects from that which characterised the former communist party states of Europe and the Soviet Union. The first is that the CCP has presided over a rapidly growing economy. There has been a rising standard of living, not just since 1978, but over the whole period of the People's Republic of China. The second is that, with only two or three exceptions, there are few regional challenges within China to the 'state-idea' of China as a whole. Unlike the USSR or Yugoslavia, the unity of the state has a long history. Its provinces have been determined by the circulation of people, goods and ideas in each locality over some two thousand years, and not by some twentieth-century notion of nationalism and administrative fiat. The exceptions — Tibet, Xinjiang and Inner Mongolia — are precisely those non-Han areas with their own independent traditions which do not share China's 'state-idea'.

China's political economy changed dramatically during 1979-1982. In those years the sheer political will of the leaders of the CCP forced through a major reform that later defeated their communist counterparts in Europe and the Soviet Union. They removed the stranglehold of heavy industry on the economy by diverting sufficient investment into light and consumer industry. The amount was not fantastically large — it is estimated at only some 3-4% of GNP — but it has significantly influenced élite-level politics, altered the trajectory of national economic planning, and resulted in the development of a consumer society, with all the attendant political as well as social and economic implications.

This is not to say that China has solved all the problems of the transition from state socialism, or indeed other problems not faced in the former Soviet Union and

Eastern Europe. Indeed the very success of economic growth creates problems, not only by creating a revolution of rising expectations, but also because economic growth in China has come about through diversity and has been sustained through allowing the market to operate, rather than government action, at any level. There appears to be a crucial disjuncture between economic growth and the political system which still emphasises, at least formally, centralisation, ideological conformity and the CCP's control of certainty.

It is from such perspectives that the experience of other East Asian societies may be of assistance. In general modernisation in East Asia can be regarded as a form of late capitalist development in which — as with Germany and Japan in the nineteenth century — the state plays a leading role. Late developers have the obvious advantages of being able to draw on the earlier experiences of their predecessors. They do not need initially to develop their own technologies for these can be imported, particularly if their economies are sufficiently internationalised. In addition, development strategies focus on production for the export market, with appropriate measures of protectionism.

Economic growth is linked inextricably with an authoritarian political system which is able to direct the mobilisation of resources to the national goal of modernisation. As the economy develops and social complexity increases then the state has to adapt to internalise the new social forces it creates. However, the experiences of South Korea, Taiwan and even Japan suggest that such transformations of régime can occur peacefully, in contrast to the violent nineteenth-century revolutions that marked the political economy of change in Western Europe. It can even be argued that, in South Korea, Taiwan and Japan, régime change has occurred without fundamentally threatening the state, leaving its authoritarianism intact.

The usefulness of regarding China as an example of East Asian late capitalism is relatively obvious, not least to the leadership of the CCP. As already noted, since the late 1980s the CCP has promoted an image of China precisely in that mould, with an emphasis on successful economic modernisation and authoritarianism as somehow more 'Chinese' than the chaos and lack of social harmony that is bound to result from Western-imported democracy. Newspaper and journal articles, as well as films and television programmes, have internalised the message to a high degree, and there can be little doubt that such instinctively reactive nationalism strikes strong popular resonances.

Throughout the twentieth century those seeking change in China have articulated a desire for a fundamentally Chinese modernisation. For many the CCP still represents the best hope of achieving that nationalist goal. Even for those who, like their earlier counterparts in the Soviet Union and the former communist party states of Eastern Europe, have become totally disillusioned with its activities and only provide support out of cynicism or an instinct for survival, the CCP may still represent the best hope for maintaining national unity or preventing the total breakdown of law and order.

From the perspective of East Asian late capitalism it seems possible that the PRC's political future might involve a slow and gradual transformation in a similar fashion to the development of politics in Taiwan and

South Korea. Were this to be the case then the state's dominance of society and its leading position in the economy is likely to remain a central characteristic of its political economy. Its political institutions are likely to be dominated by the nexus of relationships described by business, bureaucracy and politicians, and their access to wealth, power and status. Under those conditions the number of political parties engaged in electoral competition hardly impinges on the range of strategic choices available. China would thus remain dominated either by the CCP or some successor institution which provided the essential framework for the exercise of economic as well as political power.

While something similar may occur in any given locality, the diffusion of state power is already such that China is more likely to be compared to a series of Taiwans or South Koreas in the future rather than a single essentially centralised political system.

China's experience is significantly different from its East Asian late-capitalist neighbours in ways that may well influence the political consequences of social and economic change, not only domestically but also internationally. Its size is a relatively obvious but frequently underestimated difference. China is massive and this has always created problems for political control and economic direction. Even during the period of greatest Soviet influence China had a higher degree of decentralization: policies were rarely set centrally with no room for local adaptation. Economic regionalism, entailing a high degree of local variation in national policy and even local regulation, is well developed in the south and east and has to increase with economic growth.

At the same time, the decentralization of both economic management and government has been matched to some extent by the evolution of the CCP's activities. CCP organisation is now extremely localised, though it is a moot point whether its real strength locally is as much political as social. One reason the new industrialists and entrepreneurs remain keen to join is because the local CCP functions as a meeting point, facilitating social and economic rather than political ends.

China's size and regionalism are also significant because of the role it comes to play consequently in East Asia. China is so big that a relatively little growth, such as occurred during the 1980s, was sufficient to create a huge magnet for investment in the region, adding an extra dimension to international relations in East Asia. Moreover, the economic regions that have developed within the PRC are also increasingly becoming economically integrated with other specific parts of the East Asia region. Thus, Guangdong should perhaps for some time have been regarded as Greater Hong Kong; Fujian's industrial development is almost three-quarters sourced from Taiwan; Japan and Taiwan investors are particularly active in Shanghai, Zhejiang and Jiangsu Provinces; and Korean involvement is significant in both Shandong and Northeast China.

The Overseas Chinese are the major vehicle for the PRC's economic integration with East Asia and the existence of that diaspora also marks a further significant difference from other examples of East Asian late capitalism. There are some 55 million ethnic Chinese throughout the Asia Pacific region, with an additional unknown number of people of Chinese descent. The existence of

Taiwan and Hong Kong has clearly influenced the way the PRC's economy has developed, and they are likely to play a central role in the future of domestic as well as international politics.

Of course, Hong Kong will become part of the PRC in 1997, but in the meantime the process of adaptation continues as much from the PRC side as from the Hong Kong side. In addition, meeting the challenge presented by both Hong Kong and Taiwan is something that concerns the CCP and generally has driven change in the PRC since the late 1980s. An obvious example is the way the popular music scene has been drastically liberalised through the introduction of Hong Kong 'Canto-pop' and Taiwanese popular music.

There is, then, not only nationalism, but also supernationalism at the heart of China's economic growth and political transformation. One of the great ironies in the CCP's international stance after June 1989 was that, at the same time it was protesting loudly about 'harmful' Western cultural influences fomenting rebellion in China, it was permitting an influx of the kinds of popular music it would previously not have permitted. In fact 1989 marked a turning point in the PRC's policies towards East and Southeast Asia, which further increased the involvement in China of Overseas Chinese from those communities. In the aftermath of Western reaction to its suppression of the demonstrations in Tiananmen Square, the PRC quickly moved to resolve its outstanding diplomatic problems in the region, enabling the not inconsiderable Chinese business communities of Thailand, Malaysia, Indonesia and Singapore to invest in and trade with China. China's surge to economic superpower status may have started with the involvement of Hong Kong and Taiwan on the mainland in 1987, but it took off with the economic opportunities presented in the second half of 1989.

The impact of this super-nationalism on China's politics are far from certain, not least because they are not solely dependent on developments within the borders of the PRC. Within China the impact of decentralization, regionalism and international economic integration seems to indicate the greater diffusion of political power in the absence of strong leadership. Increased economic interaction and a domestic division of labour might strengthen economic integration and political unity.

However, at present the pattern of economic development suggests the opposite. Inter-provincial trade appears to have been falling for some time, though inter-provincial investment clearly has not. In fact, through international economic integration — specific to each economic region — China's provinces are becoming more rather than less autonomous, at least in relation to central government. On the surface there is a distinct possibility of an effective federalism in practice, though not in name or legally, not least because of the absence of a tradition of a rule of law. Chinese culture has long been polycentric; it was only the rigid conformism of the late Qing Empire and the state under Mao Zedong that sought to portray its centralist aspects. There are no obvious mechanisms, however, that will permit the CCP as currently constructed to manage the transformation to a new form of federalism.

How change might happen

C ONSIDERATION of the long-term trends in China's development may provide a somewhat misleading image of stability. Modernisation has rarely, if ever, proved an even or planned process. Already, as a result of its boom-bust cycles during the 1980s and the political consequences, China has proved that it is to be no exception. Rapid economic transformation has been accompanied by social dislocation and political uncertainty, the influence of which, particularly in the short-term, may be disproportionate in China's emergent politics.

The uncertainties of the rapidly changing environment are likely to be magnified by the death of Deng Xiaoping. Deng may have held no formal position of power in the structures of the CCP or the state, but he remained the undisputed 'paramount leader' of China. Even in highly institutionalised political systems uncertainties about leadership may destabilise. In political systems determined by personalities, such as that of the PRC, the illness, ageing or death of the current leadership imposes fairly obvious strains on political stability.

Despite his role as part of a collective leadership, despite the redefinition of politics so that government is reduced in scale and range, and despite the changing CCP role in the direction of society, Deng had come to play a central role in the political system. His death removes the single most important figure in China's politics, and may thus be a catalyst for political change. From the mid-1980s on he had become at one and the same time both the main defender of the communist party state and the prime generator of sustained reform. It is unlikely that anyone else can combine close associations with all the different interests — historical as well as organisational and political — that comprise the CCP in quite the way that Deng did.

Those who populate the party-state system remain the key to if not the only organized agents of political change. However, their political attitudes and behaviour may be as determined by their practical position and function in the party-state system as any allegiance to a transcendent notion of the CCP or the PRC. They may be in the party, but their purpose is more as members of a club who join to network and gather influence, not as in the past because the CCP was itself the framework of all power. It is not exaggerating their abilities to say that the leading officials see both the need to accommodate China's new social forces and to learn from the lessons of the collapse of communist rule in the former Soviet Union and Eastern Europe.

In the provinces, the political strategies of local leaders have developed in a number of directions, not least to cover a range of eventualities. They maintain close links with central government and the CCP organisation in Beijing, particularly for the short-term; and they are busy preparing their own broader bases of support in their home province for the longer term.

Their counterparts in Eastern Europe placed themselves at the head of movements for radical change when faced by major economic problems and surrounded by the apparent attractions of democracy. However, the current provincial leadership faces different socio-economic circumstances and are surrounded by a political discourse in East and Southeast Asia that stresses the synergy between economic growth and authoritarianism. From a provincial perspective the strategy is obvious: it is not a case of *for Taiwan or South Korea read China*, but rather *for Taiwan or South Korea read Guangdong or Shanxi or Shandong*.

As elsewhere in East and Southeast Asia the military may come to play a crucial role in the transformation of China's politics. However, here too there is uncertainty, not least because the PLA is not a single political actor. It might be imagined that with the reform era and the depoliticisation of other aspects of state activity the PLA would follow suit, concentrate on becoming a more professionalised, standing army and withdraw from civilian affairs, yet remain as the final arbiter and guarantor of state power.

It is certainly the case that the PLA leadership lobbied hard for its increased professionalisation since the mid-1970s and a concomitant modernisation of its weaponry. However, it is far from clear that the PLA has completely withdrawn from civilian affairs, though its involvement has changed. Charged with existing in a market-oriented economy the PLA, or rather its various constituent units, has established a large number of enterprises, many of which have only a very tenuous relationship to military activities. PLA unit budgets are now drafted on the assumption that a certain percentage of funds and resources will be generated by commercial and economic activities.

The extent to which the PLA's economic activities may jeopardise or otherwise influence its role as a major organisational support of the party-state is far from clear. The possibility exists that parts of the PLA will still not be able to stand outside any possible civilian conflict or dispute and may to the contrary be forced to intervene either partially or in its own interests. Thus, for example, it would appear that military units have been mobilised to almost purely economic ends during the various 'commodity wars' that have developed since the mid-1980s. Economic competition with other non-military enterprises has already led PLA units in Guangdong — where roughly half of all the PLA's non-military economic enterprises are physically located — into more direct forms of confrontation.

Outside the formal party-state system — which includes the PLA — there is opposition to the CCP and its policies, but accommodation is an inherent part of political life not just for business people but even for those who seek more radical political change. On the whole, both those seeking radical reform and the CCP share to a remarkable extent a fear of social disorder. There is a common recognition that too rapid political change might jeopardise the gains in the standard of living made during the reform era.

The events of 1989 alienated intellectuals and drove many into exile, where they remain. Those who were involved in the movement for reform at the time saw themselves as within the system rather than opposed to it, and that position remains an unreconciled matter of some debate amongst those now in exile. It is possible that the opposition in exile may develop new ideas and even the organisation to represent a significant threat to the CCP at some point in the future. However, at present they face enormous structural problems. They are divided, physically separate and disparate. They are fundamentally a movement of intellectuals, and while that leads to a certain influence it remains a check on their development as a mass movement. Moreover, they are outside China and thus somewhat tainted in terms of their need to appeal to reactive nationalism.

Chinese intellectuals have flirted with Western ideas of democracy since the end of the nineteenth century, but it could not be said that notions of democracy or even civil society have developed strong foundations. For the most part when democracy was spoken of in the PRC before 1989 the meaning was either that of 'socialist democracy' — perfecting state socialism — or the 'small democracies' — freedom of choice in work, home and marriage.

Despite such symbolism as the 'Goddess of Democracy' modelled on the Statue of Liberty which appeared in Tiananmen Square in May, the demonstrations of 1989 did little directly or contemporaneously to develop a new discourse or build towards civil society. However, the 1989 movement could now develop its own mythology which may well play a role in China's political future. There is a foundation for consciousness of democracy that did not exist before and which may develop, particularly with increased exposure to the rest of the world.

Given the role of the party-state in the genesis of new patterns of economic development it would be remarkable to find the new entrepreneurs generated by China's growth since the late 1970s articulating any demand for régime change of any kind, let alone a Western-style democracy, and there is no evidence to suggest that is the case. On the contrary at this stage, as one might expect with a continually rising market, most of the energy of the new entrepreneurs is concentrated elsewhere. On the other hand, greater political activism might follow from economic difficulties or renewed political interference. Their accommodation has been bought with the promise and practice of economic freedom, not by political commitment.

The death of Deng Xiaoping may not immediately plunge the PRC into either crisis or radical transformation. However, the signs for the future of the CCP would all seem to point in one direction. Decentralization, regionalism, economic growth and international integration are all set increasingly to challenge its claims to leadership. It can only survive in its dominant position if it ceases to be the CCP and redefines a role for itself based on an acceptance of high degrees of diversity and uncertainty.

There can be little doubt that the CCP is currently undergoing considerable transformation. The new economic élites who have been recruited in the era of reform have radically different perspectives on life as well as politics to their predecessors. Though they may be only too willing to reach accommodations with the current party-state they are also part of a process which is changing it from within. There can also be little doubt that there are those within the ranks of the CCP who see the direction of the structural imperatives for change. However, the CCP remains dominated at the highest levels by a relatively small group of people and their families with no such perception of the need for fundamental change.

3. Foreign policy without Deng

WHEN Deng Xiaoping was born in 1904, China was a disintegrating empire. Its territory and pride were being sliced to pieces by rapacious neighbours and predatory great powers. At the time of Deng's death, China is being touted as having the world's largest economy within a generation and as the dominant power in Asia. Of course, the return of China's international stature is not solely due to Deng, but he is arguably more responsible than any other individual. Deng played an important part in making the communist revolution, and above all shaped the post-Mao reform process that made China far richer and stronger.

But for all that China's international position has been transformed, Deng Xiaoping was strikingly crude and relatively uninterested in international affairs. The rise of China owes little to what might be called Deng's diplomacy, and nearly everything to his successful reforms at home. Deng's legacy is a China necessarily intertwined with the outside world, but with a poor sense of strategy or understanding of modern international affairs. Deng's success has left his successors with a mammoth challenge.

Deng Xiaoping's approach to international affairs was simple. He was driven by a sense of past humiliation and an understanding that recovery requires success at home. His belief in communism was relevant to foreign policy only in that it provided what he saw as the best ways to re-build China but, when international communism fragmented and then died, Deng cast off this form of ideology to reveal a more naked nationalism. He has been regularly described by foreigners as crude and nasty in handling a range of foreigners from Brezhnev to Thatcher.

70

His vaunted pragmatism was displayed when arguing for greater openness to the outside world and when being ruthless in suppressing the human rights of his opponents despite international opprobrium.

Unlike Zhou Enlai, Deng exhibited little subtlety in handling the outside world and even less understanding of the nature of international affairs in the late twentieth century. Deng seemed not to care what foreigners thought, nor did he seem to consider other more subtle options for achieving his objectives. Zhou Enlai may well have shared many of Deng's attitudes to the objectives of foreigners, but he often saw the need for diplomatic finesse. Deng's rough and unsatisfied nationalism was the norm in the first part of the century, but meant that he had little ability to understand the 'post-modern' world of limited sovereignty of states and increasing interdependence. This legacy of a man and his country caught in a time warp will pose a fundamental challenge to Deng's successors and to the world outside China.

China's successes

NOT only has China's position in the world been transformed in Deng's lifetime, it has especially been transformed in the decade-plus since Deng assumed real control of the country. In the late 1970s China was known for the idiocy and cruelty of the Cultural Revolution and the intensity of its factional politics. This was a country that had just waged a major political campaign against the long-dead Confucius and still supported revolutionary movements around the world. Twenty years

71

later his country has the world's fastest growth rates and is the favourite of Western financiers. Many people fret about China's irredentist intentions, but Chinese officials tour the world at least speaking the language of international diplomacy.

China's success is obvious, but how much is due to Deng? In one sense, if Deng was even just the visionary (and not the practical architect) of Chinese domestic reforms, then he was crucial to making it possible for China to regain its place in the world. Without successful economic reforms, China would have remained at best a bizarre irritant beset by internal crises. But it is quite another thing to argue that Deng shaped China's rise on the international scene. A clever statesman would have made it possible for China, in the words of Douglas Hurd about Britain, to 'punch beyond its weight' in international affairs. In practice, China has punched well below its weight and has avoided a high-profile role in international affairs. A clever statesman would manage to avoid debilitating conflict where it was unnecessary and to help bring about the demise of rivals.

On the contrary, Deng led China into a senseless war with Vietnam in 1979 and foolish confrontation with Britain over Hong Kong in the 1990s. China benefitted from the end of the Cold War and the death of the Soviet Union, but played virtually no role in any of these system-shattering events in the late twentieth century. On the contrary, it often demonstrated the extent to which it too was taken unawares by such events. In short, where Chinese foreign policy was not wrong, it was passive. Whatever international stature Deng has he owes to his internal policies.

By far the single most important change in international affairs that made China's rise to potential superpower status possible was the death of the Soviet Union and the end of the Cold War. Deng had long played a major role in Chinese policy towards the Soviet Union. In the 1960s he was the man who relished the opportunity to rubbish the Soviet Union and its détente with the West. He led Chinese negotiating teams in Moscow in the end-game of talks before the formal break in 1963 and was renowned for his crude attacks on Soviet leaders and policies. While Deng was acting as part of an agreed policy led by Mao, he was long seen as naturally hostile to the Soviet Union. He had spent a short time in Moscow as a student and, according to his daughter, did not enjoy his stay. His disdain was more culturally based than grounded in an assessment of Moscow's fading revolutionary credentials and dated from at least his personal experience there in 1926.

When Deng gradually began to assert his power after the death of Mao, there was much debate in the West about the extent to which Deng was an obstacle to Sino-Soviet détente. In 1977 he had confidently told the CCP that no Soviet leader would visit China in his or the next generation, or even the generation after that. In the early 1980s, when the dying Brezhnev administration and the short-lived Andropov team showed signs of desiring détente with China, Deng clearly dragged his heels waiting to see if Moscow was serious. Deng obviously did not trust the Soviet Union and saw virtue in closer relations with the West. Unlike Western statesmen who understood that it was possible to have simultaneous détente with more than one great power, Deng clung to a crude attempt to play off one side against the other.

Deng gradually gave ground to common sense, at first in economic areas and later in the political realm as Gorbachev began to de-ideologize Sino-Soviet relations. Deng never set the pace for Sino-Soviet détente and was always seen to have been dragged into concessions and compromise by the overwhelming logic of détente. As late as May 1989, when Gorbachev came to Beijing for the first summit in several decades, Sino-Soviet relations were the least developed of any of the three sides of the great power triangle. Deng accepted that there were benefits in détente with the Soviet Union, but was reluctant to the end.

1989 was in fact 'the end' in the sense that, in the last months of the year, Sino-Western relations were transformed by the Beijing massacre in June 1989 and the death of European communism in the ensuing six months. China found that it could not turn to other communists for support because not only had it de-ideologized relations with former comrades but the comrades were now out of power. Chinese diplomacy seemed to enter an angry sulk towards the West, while seeking greater sympathy in East Asia.

China established correct but cool relations with the new governments in Eastern Europe and blamed Moscow for the demise of the communist bloc that China once reviled. As the Soviet economic crisis and political chaos deepened, China tried to support, at least rhetorically, the more conservative forces in the dying system. As Sino-Western relations remained poor and Western governments supported reform in the Soviet Union, it seemed likely that China would find itself more isolated from the

West. Chinese foreign policy was stubbornly wrong in assessing the forces of history at work.

Chinese foreign policy languished in the post-1989 doldrums, but it was soon to be shaken by the events of August 1991. The failed coup in Moscow led by conservative forces applauded by China, swiftly led to the end of communist party rule and the breakup of the Soviet Union. While China obviously was worried about the impact of the end of communism on its own wobbly communist party, it had ambivalent feelings about the end of the Soviet Union. Russia had suddenly been weakened, but great uncertainty was created around China's frontiers — some, particularly if their economies are sufficiently internationalised, might think that the Chinese empire would be the next to fall. Many conservatives in China, and most China watchers, expected China to hunker down even more in response to the August revolutions. But Deng surprised them all.

Deng was instrumental in rallying his colleagues to speed up reform rather than slow it down. It was classic, brilliant Deng. The decision was driven almost entirely by domestic calculations. Deng felt that the Soviet example demonstrated that a Party failing to produce economic goods would lose power and thus reform had to be sped up. All other concerns about geopolitics or previous attitudes to Moscow were deemed secondary to a calculation of what it took to keep the Chinese communist party in power. This was not so much an example of Deng's wise foreign policy as it was a decision about domestic policy based on a judgement about someone else's domestic policy. By putting domestic policy first, it was a form of anti-foreign policy.

From 1989 onward, and certainly by the mid-1990s, relations with Russia were seen to have been an enormous success. The nature of those relations was largely shaped by events in Moscow, but China eventually had the good sense to accept the gifts of reality. And the gifts were prodigious; Sino-Russian détente meant that for the first time in several centuries China faced no life-threatening external challenge. China was more secure than at any time since the eighteenth century. By the mid-1990s China was seen to have the upper hand in relations with a Russia still in dire economic straits. Russian military forces were shrinking and Chinese traders surged across the frontier to swamp local trade. After years of rising Sino-Russian trade, by 1994 the trade was down 30% from its highs as Russians feared the political and economic impact of Chinese domination. Russia was entreating China to open its markets to Russian arms sales and Russian engineers were working in China to help build future generations of Chinese military equipment. China was even providing loans to Russia.

Russia and China are enjoying their warmest relations in several hundred years, but will it last? From a historian's perspective, the answer must be a worried 'probably not'. Russia and China are both undergoing massive domestic experiments in reform. While China seems superficially far ahead, it remains a society yet to manage the transition from peasant to urban society, from traditional to modern. The risks of massive migrations and social disorder still lie ahead in China. Decentralization has gone much further and, although not burdened by major ethnic differences as in Russia and not for the most part looking likely to result in political disintegration, the Chinese system of government has yet to put in place methods for managing decentralization within a looser federation. As a result, Sino-Russian trade is likely to remain chaotic for some time to come. Demographics of Northeast Asia suggest that Russia will always fear being flooded by China and Chinese will covet Russian resources just across the frontier. Thus border agreements announced in the first half of the 1990s are more important for the disputed issues they chose to put on one side than for the easy parts they agreed to formalize.

Hard-headed geopolitics tells us that the decline of Russia in East Asia is not yet complete and the waxing and waning of empires will continue. If this is the shape of the future, then the current peace in Sino-Russian relations is temporary. Unless Russia wishes a long-term relationship of subservience to China, it will have to count on chaos in Chinese reforms to keep Chinese hubris and irredentism from developing. Continuing Russian assistance to China's armed forces, at a minimum, seems historically ill-advised. From China's point of view, the longer it takes Russia to get its house in order, the better. It is China's national security, and the economy of its north-eastern provinces that benefits from the current relationship.

No other single aspect of Chinese foreign policy is as obviously successful as Sino-Russian relations, but there have also been significant gains in other parts of the nationalist agenda. China may not have regained territory from Russia, but it has regained stature and security. But off the coast of southern China, territory has changed hands and is set to do so in the near future. It is rare in the modern international system for territory to change sovereignty and when it does it is usually because of the exercise of military power.

Like Mao's before him, Deng's foreign policy placed importance on regaining territory lost when China was weak. Mao picked up a few rocky outcrops in the Taiwan Straits and the South China Sea. In Deng's time further gains were made in the Spratly Islands. The territory acquired in 1988 was much like that seized in the Paracels in 1974 and was made possible by clever exploitation of specific political circumstances. In 1988, as the Soviet Union was keen to improve relations with China, Beijing calculated that Moscow would be unlikely to use force to deter or repel China from taking on a once-staunch ally in Vietnam.

China's subsequent efforts in the South China Sea have been undertaken with similar subtlety, although with less obvious success. In the 1990s China had mobilized American oil companies to explore off-shore resources in the hope that the United States would be deterred from acting against its own corporations in the region. This is not the place to detail the course of the dispute in the South China Sea, but it is important to point out that China has managed to extend its claim in the region by a cautious and clever use of the division of interests among its rivals in Southeast Asia. The divide, confuse and rule strategy is not necessarily attributable to Deng Xiaoping, but it is indicative of longer term stratagems pursued by the security and foreign policy establishment of China.

The two most important outstanding issues of China's territorial integrity concern Hong Kong and Taiwan. It is a matter of great pride for Deng that he, unlike Mao or Zhou Enlai, has been able to obtain the promise of the return of Hong Kong to Chinese rule in 1997. But as in the case of the détente with the Soviet Union, we must ask how much of the success is due to coherent and skilful policy, and how much was due to the force of external circumstances. The return of Hong Kong, and the manner in which the run-up to the handover has been handled, suggests China has been reactive and sometimes foolish, even where assisted by British policies.

The decision to negotiate the 1984 Anglo-Chinese accord on the surrender of Hong Kong was triggered by a fact of life — the leases in the New Territories of Hong Kong could not be legally extended beyond 1997 without Chinese approval. Thus Britain raised the matter of post-1997 Hong Kong and only then did China formulate a policy in response. China's reaction to having the Hong Kong problem 'sprung' upon them was knee-jerk —'this is a matter of sovereignty and on such issues we will take a firm line'.

China never considered that even the most clever of British schemes would carry on without upheaval in the colony; regaining Hong Kong was first and foremost a matter of national pride, and only secondarily a question of economic benefit and political stability. Given such visceral reactions, and given China's overwhelmingly powerful position, there was little choice but for Britain to agree to hand over Hong Kong. Within these confines of power politics, it was a minor triumph of British diplomacy for Britain to coax China in negotiations between 1982 and 1984 into agreeing on mechanisms to guide the transition.

To the extent that it is possible to know what transpires in policy circles in Beijing, the best estimates suggest that Deng Xiaoping was crucial in setting the broad strategy for re-taking Hong Kong, and out of the loop on specific matters. British negotiators, like their Soviet colleagues twenty years earlier, reported that dealing with Deng on the issue was nasty and brutish. Even Mrs Thatcher, not known to shrink from diplomatic combat, was shaken by her encounter with Deng. But Deng only found himself in this place because he happened to be in power when Hong Kong's leases beyond 1997 came up for consideration. Britain always knew that China could have Hong Kong back whenever it wanted, but it saw no need to bother until someone else raised the matter. Had Mao died ten years later, it is he who would have recovered Hong Kong and not Deng.

This is not to diminish the achievement of Hong Kong's retrocession, but it is to suggest that Deng used brute force rather than diplomatic skill to attain his objectives. Even if he was not the right man, he was 'in the right place at the right time'. The extent to which he was perhaps the wrong man in the right place became more evident in the 1990s when British policy, having conceded the main point of sovereignty, became more robust in resisting the Chinese steamroller style of diplomacy. When the newly appointed Governor Chris Patten proposed mildly more democratic electoral arrangements for Hong Kong before 1997 and persisted despite Chinese opposition, Chinese diplomacy found it hard to react with anything less than a blunderbuss. All kinds of offensive language and an even wider range of dire consequences were threatened if Britain did not withdraw its proposals.

The strategy was plainly to scare the people of Hong Kong into forcing a British capitulation as in the 1982-84 negotiations. It did not work.

Hong Kong had grown more politically sophisticated especially after the events of 1989. Beijing's interests were not the same as those of southern Chinese, and Britain had a different Governor. By 1994, when Beijing realized that it had failed to browbeat Hong Kong and Britain, it settled for a policy that wiser diplomats might have adopted right from the start. China simply made plain that it would undo the reforms put in place by Governor Patten. Chinese weakness and foolishness was exposed by its frazzled rhetoric and unfulfilled threats.

Come 1997, China will obtain the return of Hong Kong, although the condition of the colony is yet to be seen. What seems less likely is that the major prize, the return of Taiwan, will take place. The crudeness of Chinese policy in Hong Kong is part of the reason for China's gradual loss of Taiwan. Far more important is the growth of an indigenous democracy in Taiwan and a vibrant economy increasingly interdependent with the global market economy. For Deng and the Beijing leadership as a whole, it was enough to proclaim the doctrine of 'one country two systems' and let an idyllic Chinese nationalism take its course. Taiwan was bound to return to the motherland. Beijing felt if it took a sufficiently robust line in not ruling out the use of force to regain Taiwan and in forcing other states to abandon recognition of Taiwan, then Taiwanese leaders would eventually capitulate.

In reality, the people of Taiwan grew in self-confidence and are increasingly finding ways of entrenching their de facto independence. China's crude diplomacy and its crass handling of domestic opposition leads Taiwanese to pull farther away from the mainland. Deng had clearly put too much faith in a simplistic vision of nationalism when Taiwan had gained too much from learning to live in the post-modern world. Deng believed that opening up China to Taiwan would bring the two closer together. Instead, it has convinced even those on Taiwan who were somewhat nationalistically sympathetic to the mainland that reunification is both unlikely and unnecessary.

The Taiwan case suggests that where Beijing lacks the resources of force majeure, its paucity of diplomatic skills or a sophisticated understanding of the international system makes it difficult to get what it wants. It is easy to win and appear clever when the cards are stacked in your favour, as in the case of Hong Kong, but far harder when the game is more evenly balanced. China even appears to have trouble punching below its weight, and until recently has not even realized that it had a problem. This crude strategy is largely the result of an excessive concern with settling nationalist scores and a remarkably poor understanding of the post-modern international system. It could also be that China simply found it difficult to have much empathy for the position of other states, at least until it feels it has re-ordered the international system.

China and the flies

MAO was kind enough to leave his successors with formal sanction to develop relations with the West. It was Mao who entertained President Nixon in 1972 and opened the gates to a stream of Western visitors. But by the time of Mao's death in 1976, China was only open to the West in the diplomatic sense. It was Deng Xiaoping who opened China in the more far-reaching sense of allowing China to become interdependent with the international market economy. While Deng knew that what he called 'flies' would come in the open door to the West, he thought that China could control the flow and nature of the insects. If Deng was serious about modernizing China he was surely correct to let the West into China, but then he was just as surely wrong to believe that China could control the infectious influence of the West.

When Deng assumed effective power in 1978, China's foreign trade totalled $20b which was 9% of GDP. Fifteen years later, China's total foreign trade was more than 7 times higher and the ratio of trade to GDP was nearly 7 times higher. China had become the world's tenth largest exporter and the second largest in Asia. By 1993 the United States had its second largest trade deficit with China and the EU had China ranked third. But by the early 1990s it was clear that China's interdependence with the international system was not simply that of one country finding a niche in the wider world. China's economic growth was based on decentralization of economic power and, not surprisingly, its interdependence was also decentralized along similar lines.

As the economic reforms gathered momentum, it became clear that many provinces, especially along the coast, were growing more interdependent with the outside world than they were with the hinterland of China. What is more, these coastal regions in China began establishing especially strong trade relations with neighbouring regions. Southern China developed closer ties to Hong Kong and Taiwan, eastern China did the same with Japan and Korea, and north-eastern China established closer relations with the Russian far east. Even south-western and western China developed closer relations with the countries across the frontier, though not always driven solely by economic rationalism. The result was a pulling at the fabric of China.

The pulling power was made possible by the fact that such interdependence with the outside world gave coastal regions greater economic ability to resist central control. Periodic attempts were made to reign in the regions, but to little avail. The most notable failure came in the second half of 1993 when Beijing gave Zhu Rongji the task of cooling the overheated economy and getting a grip on the money supply and tax system. The near complete failure of the effort to reassert central control was entirely predictable in an economy that had developed such complex links with the external world and in a political climate of uncertainty in anticipation of the succession to Deng Xiaoping.

It had been Deng's assumption that the open door to the West could be swung on its hinges when necessary. In the 1980s when the extent of economic interdependence was not yet well entrenched, it was more or less possible to yank the door closed. But by the late 1980s and especially in the early 1990s, the open door could no longer be controlled; in fact, what was once a single door now had the characteristics of a stable door. The bottom portion might be closed by a central government that controlled certain aspects of economic policy, but the top portion was beyond central control and, when open, allowed a gale to blow through.

Nor was the open door confined to economic policy. Western influence, whether in the form of political ideals or alternative lifestyle, was a major export to China. In this area, as in economic relations, Beijing believed that it could control the flow of influence. For much of the 1980s China seemed able to clamp down on dissidents, more or less as deemed necessary by Beijing officials. In 1989, when opposition to the régime was manifest in its millions on the streets of China's cities, it was clear that the protests took advantage of the fact that foreign eyes were watching China and limited the ability of the régime to act ruthlessly. The fact that student protestors raised the ultimate symbol of Western political ideals, the American Statue of Liberty, also suggested just how important were the foreign influences on China. Of course, in 1989 the régime was, barely, able to reassert political control by use of massive force. But because the régime could not clamp down economically for fear of shutting down the economic growth necessary to retain legitimacy, the essential engine of political opposition was left untouched.

As the economic engine revved in the 1990s, political problems returned. Foreigner's complaints about human rights in China have been a feature of China's foreign relations for decades, and were at their most intense in the immediate aftermath of the Beijing massacre in June 1989.

Deng Xiaoping calculated, to some extent correctly, that the West's concern with human rights would fade with time and the lure of economic opportunity. While it was true that Western governments gradually paid less attention to China's human rights policies, Deng was wrong in his belief that the matter would fade entirely. In the minds of Western populations and many government officials, China remained an unfriendly place ruled by ruthless leaders. As was the case with Western images of the Soviet Union, in the long run such images have an effect in shaping a Western policy that seeks more gradual ways to undermine the undesirable régime.

Just as in the case of the struggle with communists in Eastern Europe, so it was in the case of China that the most effective measures undermining the régime came from broader societal influences. Western influence in the form of 'alternative lifestyle' became available through foreign broadcasts and increasing contact through travel. Beijing promulgated formal restrictions on satellite dishes that receive foreign broadcasts, but the rules were openly flouted and not enforced. Even the most myopic visitor to China could see that Western cultural influences were infecting China's urban population and especially its young. While such trends do not simply translate into support for dissidents, evidence from other authoritarian régimes suggests that it does translate in the long term into weaker authority for the autocrats.

As the authority of the régime was undermined by foreign forces, the structures of power began to crumble from the inside. Corruption has existed in one form or another in the communist Chinese system even during the most radical days of the Cultural Revolution. But in the 1990s when the monetary stakes became so high, the levels of corruption, especially among the élites, scaled new heights. The open door meant that not only could money flow in to China to feed avarice and undermine authority or even just plain good government, but hot money could also flow out. By 1994, it was estimated that some $15 billion a year was leaving China in illegal efforts to feather foreign nests. An important part of the boom in the Hong Kong stock market in 1993-94 was the result of money from China seeking a safe haven. A Chinese Central Bank official admitted in 1994 that more Chinese money came into the United States than was invested by Americans in China. As the open door swung both ways, it was clear that not only were officials in Beijing not controlling the situation, but in fact they and their children were part of the problem.

Of course an important reason why such problems were tolerated was because of the benefits of interdependence. Foreign trade and investment were important parts of the engine of economic growth. The ability to raise continually the living standards of the Chinese people was a great success for Deng's régime. Growth rates, however uneven, were appreciated around the country. Differential growth caused resentment and corruption fuelled it even faster, but the reality that all could see was that trickle-down economics did trickle just about everywhere in this vast country. Such success was unknown in China for many centuries. The bottom line was that the legitimacy of the régime was hostage to relations with the outside world, while for foreigners, trade with China was of growing importance, but remained marginal.

This interdependence resulted in the increase in importance and complexity of Western policy towards China. Unlike the Soviet Union during the Cold War, China has rarely been a front-page story. During the Chinese crisis in the spring of 1989, China policy was of high priority, but the subsequent collapse of communism in Eastern Europe rapidly moved it to the inside pages. The death of the Soviet threat has cleared more space for horror stories about China selling the organs of its executed dissidents, but by and large China is most often reported on the business pages. Chinese policies are only headline news in Asia where the proclivity is to be less hostile, at least in public, about Chinese intentions.

Deng Xiaoping's rule has left a China that is perceived as more important than in 1978, but not necessarily more constructive. Interdependence was a challenge faced by many other states as they sought prosperity, but by and large they adjusted to the international system more than they reshaped it. Access to foreign markets required openness to foreign exports and influences. China has so far gained access but has resisted attempts, whether through the GATT negotiations or bilateral talks, to open its markets or to obey international rules. China has often perceived attempts to force reciprocity as part of an effort to undermine central authority, when in fact the reality has been more often the opposite, certainly when the trade problem concerns regional enterprises. Beijing often sees demands for openness as akin to demands for greater human rights, when the two issues are only connected in the loosest form. But Beijing is correct that, in the end, its acceptance of economic interdependence cannot be separated from its acceptance of greater external influence on

China's political and social system. In the end, Deng was right to choose interdependence, for to have failed to do so would have made it all the more likely that Deng would have lived to see the end of his régime, much like Gorbachev.

By choosing a policy of interdependence, Deng and his régime have survived. But the cost in the longer term must be paid. How will Deng's successor's deal with the outside world that is linked to China in ever tighter and thicker bonds of interdependence?

Where to now?

EVEN if Deng was not as important in making foreign policy as he was in making domestic policy, his death will still make a difference. It is not a difference derived from the fact that his successor has alternative ideas for, as best as one can tell, the anointed successors would wish to change little. Nor would one expect a vast difference if the likes of Zhao Ziyang should return, for he too was once Deng's protégé. The main difference, at least in the short term, will be that Deng's successors do not carry his clout within a highly personalist political system and they operate in an international system undergoing major change and increasingly able to constrain China through bonds of interdependence.

Assuming that China does not formally fragment into warring factions, the fact that the successors will be a weaker leadership cohort means that the importance of decentralized power within China, and the 'power' of the international system will be stronger. In short, it will be harder to distinguish anything that might constitute a coherent and effective Chinese foreign policy. Whether this is 'good' or 'bad' for the outside world depends on the issue at stake and the actors concerned. As China grows in importance, the already vast range of issues is expanded even further. The choices China makes matter on everything from territorial disputes to great power relations through to the nature of interdependence. It is no exaggeration to say that if China mismanages the challenges of interdependence then it puts at risk the entire East Asian region and the region's prospects for security and prosperity. For those who assume a stable and prosperous Pacific is a key to global prosperity, the stakes are high.

Territorial Issues

IT has been a truism of taxi drivers in Hong Kong that the best thing that Deng could do was to die well before 1997. The wisdom in this truism was that Deng had done much of what he could do to modernize China and set it on a course of interdependence. What was needed was a light touch by governments and some stability derived from the knowledge that the succession in China had gone smoothly.

The insecurity about the future will nevertheless remain for some time, regardless of the succession. A wise successor will allow Hong Kong to enjoy the freedoms formally promised in the Anglo-Chinese joint declaration of 1984, but few expect the future to be so rosy. The result of the row about Governor Patten's introduction of greater democracy for Hong Kong in 1993-94 was a promise by China to undo the reforms when they take over. China can be expected to attempt to fulfil this promise, with all the attendant damage to confidence in the colony.

What is more, as the economic linkages between the mainland and Hong Kong grow, the problem with corruption and the absence of the rule of law grow apace. An overly corrupt and unimpartially regulated business environment will damage Hong Kong's future. It would take a strong and brave Chinese leader to admit that the best thing for Hong Kong would be to allow it to set the pace for China, both in terms of market economics and democratic politics. Nationalism and hubris are likely to prevail, especially for a new leadership seeking to demonstrate credentials of power and adherence to core values. Thus the wisdom of taxi drivers is wrong, because Hong Kong can now expect a rougher time in 1997.

Another version of the future common on the cocktail party circuit in Hong Kong is that the weaker successors to Deng will allow Hong Kong to exert its natural leadership role in southern China. The chatter goes on to suggest that, since the Hong Kong tail already wags the Guangdong dog, and since Guangdong is so important to the prosperity of all China, Hong Kong business circles have it within their power to play a major part in the control of the Chinese economy. This scenario envisages continuing weakness in Beijing and a highly decentralized system of government. While there are many good reasons for believing that this form of fragmented and fragile Chinese government may well emerge, it is far from certain that it is good for Hong Kong.

Many might agree that the only way to govern

modern China is in a looser, more de facto federal system, but the problem is that the bases of such federalism are a long way from being in place. Federalism is usually a law-governed arrangement arbitrated by an independent judiciary. What we have in China is the crumbling remnants of an authoritarian system ruled primarily by personality and smoke and mirrors: the centre pretends to rule the regions and the regions pretend to be ruled by Beijing. The risk must be that a weak leadership will seek to assert authority with a show of strength in Hong Kong, which will bring it into conflict with regional economic and political interests. This would be even more important and a certainty if the CCP were replaced. The roots and needs of nationalism run deep. Officials in Beijing will probably seek to make an example out of Hong Kong so as to manage dissent at home, and this despite the obvious adverse consequences it will have for the prospects of reunification with Taiwan or general relations with the West. It should be obvious that the priority, at least in the short term, will be to assert control at home, no matter what the impact may be abroad.

If Hong Kong looks set to suffer, at least in the medium term, the impact on Taiwan is likely to be that much better. The key difference is that China in effect controls the fate of Hong Kong, but only aspires to control the fate of Taiwan. The more Hong Kong is damaged, the more Taiwan will seek to go its own way. Taiwan has already taken major strides towards de facto independence, having achieved this status in economic terms some time ago. As Taiwan found in the 1990s that it could have the benefits of economic cooperation with the mainland without surrendering to Beijing, the risks in continuing de facto independence seemed less great. In 1994, when Taiwan abandoned its formal claim to rule the mainland, the main question became whether the government on the mainland would evolve in a way that would offer the people of Taiwan some benefit in reunification. As Taiwan grew more democratic in the 1990s, the standards necessary for Beijing to reach became even more difficult to achieve. Would the succession to Deng make any difference?

No one expects the succession to Deng to produce an immediately democratic China. Indeed, were that to happen it would almost certainly spell problems for national politics, as the example of democratic forms without democratic culture in Russia has demonstrated only too clearly. In fact only the most wildly optimistic suggests that China could achieve anything like the standards of democracy in Taiwan for at least a generation. No successor to Deng could promise more autonomy than Deng already sanctioned, and yet even Deng's fine words have proven inadequate to a suspicious Taiwan. The change in the rules for Hong Kong as the colony grew more democratic can only inspire fear in Taiwan. Certainly no successor to Deng will promise to abandon the desire for reunification with Taiwan, and therefore the struggle looks set to continue.

The immediate risk must be that, as Taiwanese politics develop and independence becomes more formalized, a Chinese leader with a chip on his shoulder, and pushed by a conservative military lobby, will seek to halt the Taiwanese democratic process through the threat of force.

The threat of force is most likely to be realized in the

neighbouring dispute concerning the South China Sea. The policies during the Deng era clearly sanctioned the wisdom of the use of force when political costs could be minimized. Given the powerful voices in China arguing that there are good geoeconomic reasons for China to pursue a more maritime strategy, it is likely that China will continue its push for greater control of maritime resources and control of sea lanes.

For a country set to become one of the world's major importers of energy and food, the maritime imperative will be argued with increasing vehemence. The belief that China is the rightful owner of the disputed territory is not questioned within China, even though certain interests might favour a more cautious approach to the use of force. So long as China's neighbours scurry for cover each time the Chinese elephant plants its foot one step further, Chinese leaders will see little reason to halt their lumbering advance.

Although some Southeast Asians have placed their hope on a successor to Deng being more pragmatic and avoiding confrontation, the reality is that Southeast Asian governments offer little in the form of confrontation. Pragmatic Chinese leaders will value and seek out resources rather than trust in the goodwill of foreigners.

In short, the succession to Deng is unlikely to resolve any of the outstanding territorial problems. The agenda will be set by the clock ticking towards 1 July 1997, by the democratic politics of Taiwan, and by the vicissitudes of politics in a weaker Beijing leadership. Under these circumstances, a major fear must be that Beijing will find great temptation in the appeal to nationalism as a unifying force. Given the delicately poised politics in Hong Kong,

Taiwan and the South China Sea, Deng's death could not come at a more dangerous time.

Great Power Politics

DENG Xiaoping inherited Chinese foreign policy in the relatively simple atmosphere of the Cold War, but his death comes in the far more difficult, fluid environment where there was no pattern to the international balance of power. The challenge that Deng's successors will face is, in many ways, more formidable than anything ever faced by China. To be sure, there are no obvious external threats and China is more secure from such threats than at any time since the early nineteenth century. In short, China will have little problem deterring external threats. But before 1800 there was little in the way of a powerful international system to restrict Chinese behaviour. Today China is likely to have enormous problems trying to compel others to do as it wishes. Before the seventeenth century China never faced any persistent and powerful challenges in its regions. There was nothing like the European state system where relatively balanced powers were forced to accommodate the interests of other states. When China was strong it was the hegemonic power, and no one could do anything about it.

Thus the lifting of the overlay of the Cold War, and the removal of the much thicker carpet of European domination of East Asian international relations, does not have to mean that the region is headed 'back to the future'. A strong China does not necessarily have to get its own way, at least not if the other powers wish to resist. The enormous challenge for Chinese great power diplomacy is to weaken the resistance of other powers so that China can operate with relatively little hindrance. The task calls for skilful diplomacy that may not be available in a China too paranoid about its own weaknesses and with a boulder on its shoulder about the way the international system has treated it in the past.

From a geopolitical point of view, China can be seen as a continental power wishing to extend its influence outward into maritime regions in order to ensure it can retain access to increasingly needed raw materials and trade routes. Maritime states, most notably the United States and Japan, will be challenged by the extension of Chinese power. They, along with the states of Southeast Asia, can make room for China and not contest its desire for greater influence (and territory), or they can resist China and help shape a more cooperative interdependence. China does not have the military capability or the interest in extending its influence as far as the Soviet Union did during the Cold War. But China's influence in the vital East Asian region is greater than that of the Soviet Union in Europe, and certainly China's international economic power is set to be far greater than the Soviet Union could have ever realised. In order for China to increase the likelihood that the maritime world will try to appease rather than contain China, there is a need to advance Chinese interests with stealth and apparent benevolence.

The outlines of such a strategy were already apparent in Deng's dying days. When the outside world suddenly awoke to the real size of the Chinese economy and its potential to deploy massive military power, China did its best to play down its success and play up its status as a developing country. When the international community tried to draw China into webs of interdependence, China claimed it was still at a low point on a learning curve about multilateralism and therefore the rules of the game had to be bent to accommodate China. When trading partners demanded access to Chinese markets, China claimed it deserved special treatment or threatened to further restrict access to what was seen as the world's next great untapped market. China openly called for it to be given a 'breathing space' to develop its domestic base in peace and without interference.

Currently the strategy is working, but it is also increasingly hard to sustain. Reactions among the great powers to China differs and therefore offers China an even greater opportunity to grow unhindered. On one end of the spectrum of resistance to China is Russia, a power so weakened, especially in East Asia, that it has little choice but to get on with China. After decades of difficult relations, Russia is now keen to trade with China and to join the East Asian boom in part through a close relationship with China's northeast. But the challenges that lie ahead seem formidable, both for China and Russia.

Both sides will wish to trade across the frontier, but China has the upper hand because its economy is more successful. Russians will fear being swamped by Chinese traders and being dependent on the Chinese economy. With a thinly spread population sitting atop valuable natural resources, Russians must fear that its neighbours covet its wealth. Russia has no prospect of close military allies in the region and will have to look after itself in inhospitable conditions. As China grows strong, Russians will no doubt reconsider whether they wish to help arm the Chinese and help develop a modern Chinese defence industry. The legacy of historical conflict suggests it would be foolish for Russia to arm such a huge potential enemy.

From China's point of view the challenge is to kid the Russians for long enough so that the north-eastern provinces find useful trading partners and Chinese military power can be modernized. Eventually China will have to persuade Russia that the best it can hope for in East Asia is a subservient relationship to China. It will try to undermine the basis for cooperation between Russia and Japan, even though such competition is a logical strategy for a Russia that in the future might identify China as the main limit on its East Asian role.

Similarly, China must persuade Russia that the United States would be an unreliable partner in East Asia. Russia could be a useful partner with the maritime powers in containing China, but for the time being difficulties in Russo-Japanese relations have helped encourage Russia to choose closer relations with China. To an important extent, China's ability to persuade Russia to stay on its side of the fence depends on events in Russian and Japanese domestic politics that are well beyond Beijing's control. Since the task for Chinese leaders will be to keep Russia friendly, clever Russian leaders will play on China's fear of closer Russo-Japanese relations as a way of limiting Chinese control of Russo-Chinese relations.

This tightly knotted pattern of great power relations depends to an important extent on directions of change in Japan. Tokyo's view of Sino-Japanese relations has been based on a quietly held assumption that China could be controlled because it was weak and dependent on Japanese technology. But in the dying days of the Deng Xiaoping régime, Japan grew less confident about this calculation at the same time as its domestic politics began major reforms. Those Japanese reforms are still not completed and the Japanese have not consolidated a new view of China.

As a result, the way China handles Japan is delicately poised. Current trends suggest that Japan is coming to view China as less controllable and more of a long-term challenge. Just as Japan's economy looked set to power ahead and catch up to the United States, it stalled, and China's GDP, calculated on the controversial basis of purchasing power parities, moved ahead. Japan never got to be No. 1 and now looks set never to rise above No. 3. The shock to the Japanese system, as well as various other post-Cold War changes, is leading it to become more assertive and perhaps more nationalist. It was long thought that the target of such assertive nationalism would probably be the United States, but geopolitical logic suggests another option.

What is more likely is a Japan increasingly fearful of a powerful and vengeful China. Such a Japan would be likely to seek closer relations with the United States and other maritime states in East Asia. Japan would seek to trade with China, but it would be cautious about the technology it transfers. Japan would also increasingly find its trade focused on China's northern coastal regions as local webs of interdependence are woven. Japan may not have a vested interest in a divided China as it did in the first part of the century, but it is certainly in its interests to see a China weakened by fissiparous tendencies.

Part of the reason why China is sensitive to discussions about the impact of decentralization and regionalised politics is precisely the fear that some, like the Japanese, have in the past made a habit of manipulating such weaknesses.

The challenge for post-Deng Chinese diplomacy will be to persuade Japan that it is not a long-term challenge. China will seek to exacerbate United States-Japan frictions and at the same time hope that the United States can contain Japanese assertiveness and nationalism. Such a strategy probably calls for a China that is less critical of Japanese nationalism and harps on much less about Japanese wartime activities. Clever Chinese diplomacy will worry less about antagonizing the United States so long as it appeases Japan. Clever Chinese will understand that they now have the upper hand with Japan and can play a long game of gradual modernization that takes China well past dependence on Japan and is successfully able to manipulate the competitive instincts of the global market economy.

As Japan debates its own identity as an Asian or Western state, China will have an opportunity to help shape Japanese choices. The risk must be that a renewed Japanese nationalism will come into conflict with a rising Chinese counterpart. Under such circumstances the risks will increase that China will face a hostile maritime coalition determined to limit Chinese influence.

An important piece of the coalition would obviously be the United States, and here too there are major doubts about how domestic affairs will set priorities. The United States has 'held the ring' of the Asian balance of power, especially after the end of the Cold War. Yet the United States has demonstrated a growing reluctance since the 1990-91 Gulf War to become militarily engaged in East

Asia or anywhere else for that matter. As the United States backed off taking a firm line with North Korea, or declined to deter Chinese activity in the South China Sea, it was increasingly clear that the United States would not pursue an active military policy unless asked and assisted by local states. Left to its own devices, the United States is gradually retreating militarily from East Asia.

Such a retreat by and large suits China well. An active American military presence was useful to China in controlling the Soviet Union or perhaps even Japan. But as China is increasingly defined as the most likely hegemonic power in East Asia, there is a clear Chinese interest in a retreat of American power. An Asia left to Asians means an Asia more subject to Chinese influence. Chinese geopoliticians have thought that it is necessary to pay much attention to Sino-American relations, but that attention will decrease as does American power and influence. In the past, China has had a tendency to make the United States the centre-piece of its geostrategy, and while the United States remains important on everything from the GATT to arms control, China will need to be prepared to play the United States off against a range of other powers.

We have already suggested ways in which United States-Japan relations might be manipulated to China's advantage. Beijing might also find, especially in trade issues, that the European Union and its constituent parts are usefully manipulated to make the United States compete for China's favours and markets. The obverse of this notion is that China will have to prevent Europeans from joining with the United States and Japan in setting rules for China's good behaviour in the international system. It goes without saying that China will have an interest in a less common European foreign and defence policy and a less coherent G-7 or OECD. Some of the tasks in dividing China's opponents will be easier than others (viz. the European Union). The essence of the challenge for the post-Deng leadership is to manage a coherent and subtle foreign policy at a time when China becomes more complex and fragmented and China's rivals have an increasing need to formulate a more coherent policy to manage Beijing. The task is enormous.

Tightening Interdependence

DENG Xiaoping was not responsible for the shape of the great power balance or even the primacy of nationalism on China's foreign policy agenda, but he was responsible for the biggest challenge facing his successors in foreign policy, the challenge of interdependence. To the extent that anything is irreversible, China has no choice but to get on in an interdependent world. Once the economy relies on trade and foreign investment, the cost of giving up profits and finance is prohibitive for any successor. The only realistic circumstance under which China may become less interdependent with the outside world is if the economy or society collapses inside China. Otherwise, Deng has left a fur-lined mousetrap for his successors. The most important uncertainty about post-Deng foreign policy is how the challenge of interdependence will be met.

China is now a net food and energy importer and its deficit in these items will grow as the economy develops.

China needs foreign markets for its exports. Put these two realities together and China can be expected to run trade deficits with countries who produce primary goods and raw materials, and run a surplus with developed economies with large markets. Japan, the EU and the United States will run persistent trade deficits and therefore will have major leverage over the Chinese economy. Economic disputes with these countries, leaving aside human rights or security disputes, are likely to increase. The postwar history of EU and United States disputes with Japan and the NICs will be mild in comparison to relations with a China that makes no pretence of being an ally of the major Western trading entities. What is more, the wild economic cycles in China will be increasingly important and annoying as China becomes more interdependent with the global economy.

When we add in disputes over human rights, the environment and military issues, it is a safe bet that China's interdependence with the outside world will be fraught with problems. Multilateral arrangements, whether they be the World Trade Organisation or arms control treaties, will be tested by how they adapt to Chinese policies and demands. No other country poses such a challenge to the existing international régimes. Thus it is critical to understand how China is likely to react to multilateralism and interdependence.

The record in the Deng era is only partially encouraging. China was willing to take part gingerly in multilateralism, but did so either as a relatively passive actor (e.g. the United Nations), or as a demandeur of change (the GATT or arms control). How much longer can Chinese officials at the United Nations be known for stalling and slowing agreement among a concert of great powers? Chinese rarely shape the agenda or resolutions in any international institution. Part of the reason for such passivity is no doubt their unfamiliarity with how genuine multilateralism functions, although over time such excuses grow less convincing. Part of the reason is that, much as when the Chinese ambassador to the United Nations switches off his hearing aid, they just do not like to hear unpleasant ideas.

China knows enough to know that multilateralism is confining. Because interdependence means a degree of dependence, a China that sees itself as a non-status quo power has natural problems in accepting limits on its behaviour. Those who negotiate trade accords with China report that the Chinese simply do not understand that the idea behind interdependence is that both sides can gain from an action by one side — trade is not a zero-sum game.

The extent to which Chinese genuinely do not grasp the essentials of multilateralism and interdependence is worrying. It may be that the successors to Deng will have a more intuitive grasp of the realities of the modern international system where sovereignty can often be a Victorian value. The fact that the immediate successors were most often shaped by contact with the system in the 1950s Soviet Union does not suggest there will be a rapid change to a Western mind-set. What seems most likely is a contest of mind-sets as China is dragged towards increasingly intense interdependence, and the outside world decides how much change it wants to demand of China.

If other East Asians come to see China as a problem requiring control, they are likely to find willing partners in the more developed world. Should they choose to acquiesce in Chinese dominance of East Asia, they may find themselves increasingly caught up in a Chinese confrontation with the developed world. Given an increasing degree of Chinese interdependence, there will be ways in which the Chinese economy and society can be constrained. These constraints may be applied in part through more direct relations with important parts of a decentralized China.

The successors to Deng can choose a less confrontational approach and accept the constraints of interdependence. But because they are unlikely to do so unless the outside world shows greater firmness and coherence than it did during the Deng Xiaoping era, it is likely that Chinese leaders will opt for more nationalism and less cooperation. Sooner, but more probably later, the developed world is likely to find itself on the edge of a major confrontation with a post-Deng China.

Select Bibliography

Asia Research Centre, Murdoch University *Southern China in Transition* Australian Government Publishing Service, 1992

Joseph Cheng (ed) *China's Modernisation in the 1980s* Chinese University of Hong Kong Press, 1990

The China Quarterly Special Issue on Deng Xiaoping, September 1993.

Lowell Dittmer *China Under Reform* Boulder, Colorado, Westview Press, 1994.

J. A. Dorn and Wang Xi (ed) *Economic Reform in China* University of Chicago Press, 1991.

David S. G. Goodman *Deng Xiaoping and the Chinese Revolution* Routledge, 1994.

David S. G. Goodman and Gerald Segal (ed) *China Deconstructs* Routledge, 1994.

David S. G. Goodman and Beverley Hooper (ed) *China's Quiet Revolution* Longman, 1994

D Granick *Chinese Enterprises* University of Chicago Press, 1990.

Harry Harding *China's Second Revolution* Brookings, 1987.

Harry Harding *A Fragile Relationship* Brookings, 1992.

W. Kraus *Private Business in China* C. Hurst, 1991.

Ellis Joffe *The Chinese Army After Mao* Weidenfeld, 1987.

Simon Long *Taiwan: China's Last Frontier* Macmillan, 1991.

William Overholt *China: The Next Economic Superpower* Weidenfeld, 1993.

Thomas Robinson and David Shambaugh (eds) *Chinese Foreign Policy* Oxford University Press, 1994.

Gerald Segal *China Changes Shape* Adelphi Paper No. 287, 1994.

Gerald Segal *The Fate of Hong Kong* Simon & Schuster, 1993.

Dorothy Solinger *From Lathes to Looms: China's Industrial Policy in Comparative Perspective* Stanford University Press, 1991.

Dorothy Solinger *China's Transition From Socialism* M.E. Sharpe, 1993.

Michael Yahuda *China's Foreign Policy After Mao* Macmillan, 1983.